Bread Machine Cookbook

Hands-off Recipes for Perfect Homemade Bread

(Quick and Easy Homemade Recipes to Get Your Fresh Fragrant and Tasty Bread Every Day without Effort)

Travis Williams

Published By **Zoe Lawson**

Travis Williams

All Rights Reserved

Bread Machine Cookbook: Hands-off Recipes for Perfect Homemade Bread (Quick and Easy Homemade Recipes to Get Your Fresh Fragrant and Tasty Bread Every Day without Effort)

ISBN   978-1-998901-32-6

No part of this guidebook shall be reproduced in any form without permission in writing from the publisher except in the case of brief quotations embodied in critical articles or reviews.

Legal & Disclaimer

The information contained in this ebook is not designed to replace or take the place of any form of medicine or professional medical advice. The information in this ebook has been provided for educational & entertainment purposes only.

The information contained in this book has been compiled from sources deemed reliable, and it is accurate to the best of the Author's knowledge; however, the Author cannot guarantee its accuracy and validity and cannot be held liable for any errors or omissions. Changes are periodically made to this book. You must consult your doctor or get professional medical advice before using any of the suggested remedies, techniques, or information in this book.

Table Of Contents

Chapter 1: A Bread Machine

The bread tool, also popularly known as the bread maker, is a system or equipment located inside the kitchen created with the motive of baking raw substances into consumable bread. Bread is a kind of meals that is baked the usage of pretty some dough and can be in such a lot of wonderful patterns and sizes, as well as dispositions. Bread materials are relying at the needs of the only baking it and can be organized in hundreds of strategies, as properly. Bread is concept to be one of the global's oldest substances.

A bread tool is manufactured from a bread pan and paddles which might be included and are placed inside the middle of a multi-reason oven this is small and viable, as properly. This small oven has a integrated micro-laptop, that is what you operate to perform the bread maker. There are special settings at the bread maker, relying on the sort of bread you need to bake. These settings encompass the ones for white bread, whole bread, French bread, further to simple dough like the ones of pizzas. There is likewise an opportunity of a timer on the bread maker to permit it to head on and rancid routinely even when you aren't within the location to characteristic it.

The bread maker is essentially a smaller oven version that uses energy and that would first-class accommodate one bread pan in it. The bread pan is characterised via an axle that is located at its bottom, connecting it to a motor, run with the aid of way of power. The waterproof axle then connects to a small steel paddle. The paddle is the only that kneads the dough.

The bread maker has a lid this is every opaque or see-through, depending on the make and model. The lid additionally comes with a vent that is used to do away with all the more steam produced at some stage in the baking machine and an air vent on its side to permit air to are to be had in, this is crucial for the dough to upward push properly. It has a control panel at the pinnacle a good way to will let you carry out it without troubles.

1. Instructions on How to Use the Bread Maker

Bread makers require factors to be placed in a selected order. Most are discovered through a guide guide to will let you follow instructions and get your selected outcomes. In most bread makers, you input additives, starting with the moist materials first, followed with the aid of the dry additives subsequent. The wet materials get to move first due to the truth you will use dry yeast at the identical time as baking your bread, which dreams some water content as a manner to set off it. In a bowl for blending, supply collectively all moist components before inputting to ease the artwork. Do the same with all of the dry materials, as nicely. It is critical to word that the bread maker will take the time to make the bread, commonly a few hours at a time. Also, the order of inputting materials can also moreover variety among machines, so follow the manual instructions on your sort of device.

The bread maker works thru first settling the components that you have enter, then elevating the temperature to the desired stage. You can view the method spread if your unique bread maker comes with a viewing window. What takes vicinity next is that the elements are changed into dough through the usage of the built-in paddles; you could moreover pay attention the sounds from interior as this takes region. This is then found thru the dough developing proper right into a bread form wherein you can see steam emanating from inside the bread maker; then, eventually, it's far baked. Once the bread is prepared, you extract the bread pan and take away the bread, then set it apart to chill off in advance than cutting it.

2. Types of Bread Makers

There are hundreds of bread machines to be had inside the marketplace nowadays. The one you choose is relying at the reason you have got in mind. The kinds of bread machines encompass:

a.Vertical bread maker. This type of bread device is used for baking loaves in a vertical way, that is how the bread pan is placed and fashioned. The vertical bread maker is one type that has tremendous one kneading paddle in it.

b. Horizontal bread maker. This is the form of bread maker characterized via manner of having kneading paddles in it. This bread maker is used for baking loaves which may be horizontally fashioned and are maximum not unusual in business corporation bread making.

c.Small bread maker. Small bread makers are the maximum great to be used on your small kitchen, specifically at the same time as you bake best for your circle of relatives. They produce a small bread first-class for a own family setting.

d. Large bread maker. This sort of bread maker is right while baking for a big enterprise of human beings thinking about you may bake huge loaves of bread.

e.Gluten-loose bread maker. This is a kind of bread maker that has a setting for gluten-loose bread built in it. This is proper at the same time as you're baking wholesome loaves of bread.

3. Benefits of a Bread system

a.You get to revel in freshly baked bread right within the comfort of your home. The taste is also rich and complete of taste considering factors are not unfold among many loaves of bread like in commercially produced store-presented bread.

b. Most bread makers have a timer feature in which you could, for instance, set it to bake within the morning, and at the same time as you wake up, you could have warm bread expecting you for breakfast.

c.You get to be in rate of what you consume due to the fact you get to choose out the elements you need to use for your bread. This is proper for those humans with meals allergies and those who devour tremendous varieties of meals and refrain from exceptional sorts.

d. Baking bread using a bread maker might be very easy. All you want to do is mixture your components, positioned them into the bread pan, and choose your putting alternative.

e.A bread maker can be a long-term money saver. This is in particular authentic in case you choose fine styles of special bread with unique additives, which, while offered commercially, can be quite pricey.

f. Bread makers are built in this kind of manner that you get to bake fantastic styles of bread, depending on your desires. You can select out to bake white bread, entire bread, gluten-free bread, or numerous special bread types.

Chapter 2: Making Bread

There is not anything much like the fragrance of freshly baked bread to greet you at the same time as you wake up. Bakers historically produced their merchandise in the path of the early hours which means their loaves have been sparkling, warm, and mouth-watering tasty for hungry clients trying a slice of bread to go with a slap-up breakfast.

Bread historically dates decrease once more to Neolithic or possibly prehistoric instances in its earliest incarnation.

Prime materials encompass flour and water used to make the dough. The dough may additionally moreover have numerous components to provide diverse consistency, flavors, and healthful options. Additives might also embody yeast, fat, salt, baking soda, end result, spices, eggs, milk, sugar, or veggies. You can even upload seeds to the bread, oils, and nuts. Bread is quite a flexible product and may be wolfed on its very very personal or as an accompaniment to the precept dish. The dough is traditionally baked, however current-day options must encompass steaming.

The outer a part of the bread, usually called the crust, can be baked right into a hard or smooth version. The inner part of the bread is assessed due to the truth the "crumb," surprisingly now not the small bits that cowl your lap.

The pinnacle time to consume a loaf of bread is quick after it's miles been eliminated from the oven. At this scrumptious time, the bread is warmness, aromatic, and glowing. Leaving the bread for any term will motive the bread to come to be stale.

A quirk courting lower once more to the 13th century have become the Baker's Dozen.

A Baker's Dozen, ironic because it become from the 13th century, relates to 13 devices making a dozen in choice to the usual 1 1/2 of. As statistics would have us accept as true with, a Baker's dozen recommended that punishment have emerge as administered to bakers who brief-changed their customers. One manner to make certain that a consumer continuously obtained an entire quota turn out to be to offer greater bread than paid for. Furthermore, if one loaf end up damaged, burnt or modified into of unacceptable excellent, there were still 1 1/2 of loaves available for the purchaser.

Another explanation of the Baker's Dozen, and barely extra believable, is that once spherical loaves have been positioned on a popular baking tray, the configuration changed into three+2+three+2+three which gave a more density to the tray and allowed less complicated stacking.

Over the severa years, the baking of bread has placed the course of many traditions up to date to mirror the converting needs of society. Whereas bread grow to be generally the keep of the neighborhood baker, contemporary supermarkets now have their non-public "in-residence" ovens, and bread is baked to suit client name for.

4. How to Choose the Best Bread Maker

The current-day-day automated bread maker is a exquisite addition to any circle of relatives domestic. While product reliability and variety of skills may also moreover were in query in years long past by using the usage of, superior manufacturing standards and excessive name for for extra person-pleasant home equipment have ensured there may be an automated bread device available to match all of your dreams.

If you're looking for to buy a bread maker, you need to bear in mind numerous factors earlier than you are making your shopping for choice.

First at the listing of worries is the quantity of bread you may want to make. If you have got a large circle of relatives and feature the selection to make batches of bread to satisfy your hungry children, then there are domestic device to be had so one can will can help you make loaves up to 2.Five lb. In weight. But then again, in case you are a retired couple or a unmarried couple with confined bread needs, numerous smaller merchandise are to be had to make a 1 lb. Loaf. Having this preference proper from the start is essential because of the truth you may store cash and waste it on time. If you're searching out variety, sure producers have one-of-a-kind bread sizes in between.

User-friendliness is likewise a big issue to recollect as all gift bread machines can offer a large shape of programmable answers based absolutely on the model you may manipulate to pay for.

Of precise examine are timer capabilities that put off baking the bread to a time that suits your desires. E.G., if you need to make a bread that is handiest warm out of the oven first issue within the morning and is on a four-hour baking duration, then positive features will will allow you to load the elements in advance than going to mattress after which begin the baking manner in the midnight. This form of role places you in whole manipulate of the baking way. Many synchronized features can sound warnings even as unique substances want to be added, or even as the baking cycle is entire.

One distinct important issue to bear in mind is the product portfolio you want to offer your automatic bread maker. If it is honestly easy white or brown bread, then many easy domestic device will bake them with a minimal fuss. Be effective, but, to check out the numerous distinctive merchandise that bread makers can supply on. From the basic to the maximum superior, bread makers will make a desire of numerous quantities of bread, doughs for pizza options, lots of cake alternatives, fruit pieces of bread, or even jams.

Choosing the exquisite bread maker may be tough given all of the options on offer and the variety of producers taking walks within the marketplace these days.

5. Reasons Why You Could Want a Bread Machine

By now, maximum human beings were studying about bread machines. The call on my own gives you an idea of what you're having, a bread-making unit! Although this is real, the hazard of getting your personal is a lot more. You will keep fuel, but you will also have get right of entry to to diverse quantities of bread, which can be very purchaser-friendly.

Save Some Cash

The first gain that we are capable of be thinking about is the fee. Instead of taking walks to the grocery keep, you will be saving time with a bread machine. Loaves are in the marketplace for approximately three-5 cents and on the better end if you are selecting "sparkling" or "all-herbal" bread. You may additionally additionally moreover appearance as small as 50-75 cents a loaf relying on what sort of bread you're making and the elements.

Versatility

In a bread maker, you may make all varieties of bread. Some examples consist of banana, almond, potato, apple, and bread crafted from fruit. Gluten-free periods for those who can't tolerate Gluten gadgets are also to be had on some fashions.

Aside from baking bread, the greater current-day versions have exclusive configurations. Bread makers also can make confectionery, desserts, and meatloaf.

Even most bread makers do double duty as a way of making flour. Some human beings, having sold a bread tool, use this selection as their vital precedence. You also can create bread or perhaps give up a loaf in the oven to deliver croissants, pies, and rolls.

Easy to Use

The bread machines are very purchaser pleasant. When the bread device is washed, the materials may be weighed, positioned within the pan, the bread pan inserted into the oven, the system begins offevolved, and the bread can be baked. This is so clean. All include clean-to-use, preset bake cycles.

The Rationale for Buying a Bread Machine

If you are a fan of bread loaves, bread machines are a first-rate desire. They are rate-powerful, easy to apply, and offer a big selection of selections.

Bake a loaf, and enjoy it.

Mouth-watering Recipes for Free Bread

If you get a chunk uninterested in using your bread tool's recipes, why now not be experimental and strive new ones. Thousands of loose bread maker recipes can be located on line, and everything is a baby's play. Here are only some for whetting your urge for meals.

6. Quick Ideas to Make Bread Recipes

Did you word the breakfast bread costs recently? It's sufficient to have you ever marvel if making your very very own wouldn't be less complex. You maintain in thoughts what it is like! A big bag of bread flour and quite a few exceptional materials will produce quite some loaves. Depending on your selected recipe, you may need a few yeast, salt, sugar, butter, water, oil, and maybe an egg or .

Fast bread recipes are also a super opportunity to the antique university manner of manufacturing domestic-baked loaf. You should probable use a bread maker to do the interest for you, but you then surely definately'd be losing out on the amusing of baking the cookies yourself.

There are some subjects to hold in thoughts while getting geared up the sandwich. If you've in no manner made bread earlier than, pick a easy recipe. Prepare as a result. Read via the recipe commonly to get familiar with the substances and the way. It is crucial to comply with the recipe with precision.

Learning how to make bakery bread is a brilliant way to get commenced to your adventure inside the course of a extra in form manner of life, plus loving the easy, wet loaf that truely melts on your mouth. Yummy is the handiest time period that can nicely describe home made loaf.

There are extraordinary tactics you may make a loaf. You can bake it thru hand from scratch, or use a bread gadget to make the dough for you. The second yields right consequences, however it appears with out the "home made" best that comes from kneading and looking the loaves taking form from your personal arms.

Until you start ensuring all your assets are at room temperature. Yeast loves a heat environment. Measuring dry and wet elements is paramount in growing a gentle, tasty loaf. If you find out it useful, weigh the substances in advance.

Follow the recipe with precision. If it says in a nice order combining of the elements, do it. Bread making is as plenty a technology as an artwork, and if you need your loaf to pop out the equal every time, follow the instructions to the letter!

It's time to knead the flour till all of the materials are blended. You'll want extra flour to unfold and dip your palms on the board, so the dough does not adhere to you or the tabletop. It is vital to knead the gluten within the bread dough, mix it in the air for raising, and unfold the substances just so the yeast can devour. Yes, the yeast in the dough feeds on the sugars and creates a fermentation procedure, which lets in the dough to upward thrust well. In bread-making, the maximum crucial rookie mistakes is not kneading the dough lengthy enough. Suppose you want to use a timer. You'll want from 1 half-5minutes to knead the bread.

Form the dough right into a ball at the same time as you're completed kneading and positioned it in a greased bath. Cover and let out. Your dough may want to require 1-2 hours of sitting to upward thrust. To help the developing cycle, ensure your kitchen is dry.

You'll need to show the dough on the quit of this cycle, punch it down, shape the dough like you want it to be, bake it and cover it up for every different developing consultation. It's time to roast, developing even as achieved. Preheat the oven until it bakes. When cooking the bread, permit it cool in advance than slicing really.

When you have perfected a recipe for smooth bread, you can make artisan bits of bread, French bread, natural bread, rolls, and greater.

Chapter 3: How To Use A Bread Machine

7. Meet Your New Bread Machine

Hot golden crescents, freshly baked breakfast cakes, fragrant tea desserts, and scrumptious cakes to accompany your morning espresso. All of those may be cooked with a bread gadget in minutes and with a hint try for your element. Also, the ones scrumptious and wholesome baked objects can be made with the best and maximum common additives. The handiest precise component you want to characteristic is your love and creativity!

As for the stupid and routine duties, which includes baking, mixing, stirring, the bread tool will cope with them leaving you the great and most interesting, this is, the selection of the recipe and the selection of things. Isn't this a first-rate manner to experience the unique aroma and taste of precisely the shape of baked goods you need?

Even if you're no longer proper at the usage of contemporary home equipment, positioned your troubles behind you, due to the reality bread machines have smooth, easy-to-use controls. They are fun and smooth to use! Besides making easy bread, they also can make and knead any shape of dough, bake dough out of the box, or maybe make dough jam. When you get to recognize this available tool, it will without a doubt become an crucial and amazing beneficial resource to your kitchen.

It's so clean:

1.Insert the baking sheet into the tool.

2.Attach the dough blades.

3.Add components as demonstrated in your tool manual.

4.Close the lid.

5.Turn on the tool.

6.Select the preferred characteristic.

8. What Else Can It Do?

Different bread machines may also moreover range in their format, functionality, form of accessories, and programs to be had. When choosing your bread device, reflect onconsideration on your private options and dreams: What will you do with the device? Do you want any specific programs and extra modes, or is the simple capability sufficient?

Bread machines can knead the dough, permit it rest, bake a crunchy baguette, make candy cupcakes or unleavened bread, and plenty greater.

9. Main Ingredients

The additives wanted for bread making are quite clean: flour, yeast, salt, and liquid. Other additives upload flavor, texture, and nutrients to your bread, which incorporates sugar, fats, and eggs. The essential materials embody:

Flour is the inspiration of bread. The Protein: and gluten in flour form a network that traps the carbon dioxide and alcohol produced through using the yeast. Flour moreover offers clean sugar to feed the yeast and it provides taste, relying on the sort of flour used in the recipe.

Yeast is a dwelling organism as a manner to boom even as the right amount of moisture, meals, and heat is carried out. Rapidly multiplying yeast gives off carbon dioxide and ethyl alcohol. When yeast is authorized to undergo its life cycle really, the completed bread is greater flavorful. The super yeast for bread machines is bread tool yeast or energetic dry yeast, relying on your bread system model.

Salt strengthens gluten and slows the rise of the bread with the useful aid of retarding the motion of the yeast. A slower upward push lets in the flavors of the bread to increase better, and it will likely be much less possibly the bread will rise too much.

Liquid turns on the yeast and dissolves the possibility substances. The most typically used liquid is water, however materials which embody milk also can be substituted. Bread made with water may additionally have a crisper crust, but milk produces rich, gentle bread that gives greater nutrients and browns much less complicated.

Oils and fats add flavor, create a mild texture, and assist brown the crust. Bread made with fats remains glowing longer due to the reality moisture loss in the bread is slowed. This factor can also inhibit gluten formation, so the bread does not rise as immoderate.

Sugar is the supply of meals for the yeast. It additionally gives sweetness, tenderness, and coloration to the crust. Too a whole lot sugar can inhibit gluten increase or purpose the dough to upward push an excessive amount of and collapse. Other sweeteners can update sugar, at the facet of honey, molasses, maple syrup, brown sugar, and corn syrup.

Eggs add protein, flavor, colour, and a tender crust. Eggs contain an emulsifier, lecithin, which lets in create a steady texture, and a leavening agent, which enables the bread upward thrust well.

10. Bread Yeast

Bread Yeast is a residing organism that feeds at the dough's sugar (carbohydrates) and water and expels carbon dioxide (which office work bubbles that make the bread upward thrust) and ethanol as waste merchandise.

Much like grapes come to be wine, the dough's sugar feeds the bread yeast. The dough stays in the bread device and is supplied with warmth and liquid to be transformed into bread. As the dough rises, the yeast eats sugar and shits alcohol.

11. Different Yeasts

There are one-of-a-type yeasts available in stores that produce precise styles of bread and feature very specific roles inside the advent of bread.

Bread yeasts are categorized into groupings: speedy-rise and well-known.

Fast-growing yeasts are used in bread machines because the usage of them will growth the price at which the bread tool can shape a complete loaf of bread with out the client having to be home at midday to function extra factors, alongside side eggs, raisins, or butter.

Once the dough is located into the bread system, it's far set to upward thrust at its default pace thru turning the system on.

While the dough is growing, the yeast starts offevolved ingesting the sugar inside the dough, developing alcohol from this alcohol that releases carbon dioxide, and grade by grade, the dough rises. Rapid-upward push yeast is used in lots of bread tool recipes.

Fast-rising yeast produces instances quicker than state-of-the-art yeast and can be at once introduced into the bread tool from the package and could not require proofing.

Unfortunately, as with every cultured products, the yeast may be reduced via exposure to warmth, bloodless, and humidity.

Slow growing yeast is called for in recipes with a totally ultimate upward thrust time in the device of extra than 2 hours.

The remarkable yeast for a bread machine is bread gadget yeast or energetic dry yeast. The cells of these yeasts are quite warm temperature, cold, and sickness resistant, and could not die off whilst exposed to outdoor conditions. This is the energetic element needed to create bread inside the bread device. New yeast will despite the fact that settle out of suspension due to the fact the device runs, in desire to letting it's used to make greater dough.

New bread yeast desires to be rehydrated at an 80° to eighty five° Fahrenheit temperature for 30 to 60 mins.

12. Sourdough Yeast

Sourdough yeast isn't heated, but the sugar needs to have been previously dissolved by way of way of a proofing segment that lasts about 4 hours. Baking the dough right away will hold all the goodness of this yeast—do no longer use boxed yeast.

You will need to characteristic the yeast to the moist baking substances the use of the enclosed mixing tool due to the fact the yeast will not live on being introduced immediately to the dough. Pre-degree your yeast proper right into a small bowl.

Test your yeast and your water with a thermometer to make certain that the water is not too heat or too bloodless to aid its metabolism.

Combine your yeast with the water, stirring very well for about 30 seconds.

Use the proofing cycle to growth the temperature of the flour and yeast aggregate to approximately 80 five° to ninety 5° ranges.

thirteen. Different Flours

Different flours will supply specific merchandise whilst mixed with yeast.

When blending with yeast, one will most probable get strong belly formations, and the flavor is absolutely particular depending at the milk or butterfat contents of the dough. This is all regular.

Mixing will maintain till all the flour has been dispersed (if completed via manner of hand) as heaps as five mins. The dough can be slack and airy and the crumb may be tight and vibrant.

Place the dough within the bread device as knowledgeable on your recipe.

Check at the dough to peer what has been finished. You will no longer need to, initially, make certain the dough is of the appropriate consistency. If you've got were given introduced an excessive amount of water to the yeast-exposed flour combination, the dough may be too moist. The dough wants to be the correct consistency for the fashion of bread you need.

14. Bread Crust

Bread crusts are normally a form of crusts which may be smooth to the touch however employer to the chunk, which may additionally moreover range in texture from hard to moderate to clean. They are characterized with the resource of having a difficult floor. The crust is the outermost layer of a loaf of bread or the shell spherical every different food product.

Bread makers are business bread-making machines that can be used to make a large variety of loaf sorts. The machines essentially knead the dough of bread or rolls. Once the dough has been organized and placed inside the bread tool, the customer sets the device with the popular time, and then it's far baked later in the day.

Bread machines come each digital and conventional. For the traditional or analogs, they're slower however home made loaves may be produced with greater accuracy.

Some of the opposite food which may be made in bread machines are cakes, cakes, pizza, rolls, sandwich rolls, fish or seafood, greens, lattes, pasta, breakfast bread, or maybe pies.

Crust Too Thick

-Flour has too little gluten

When flour has little gluten, the crust has a tendency to be too thick. This is due to the flour no longer having masses of wheat protein, or the dough no longer being given sufficient kneading within the course of many ranges of manufacturing.

Crust too thick additionally can be because of the dough being too stiff (low percentage of water).

Bread Is Too Dense

-Too plenty gluten

If bread has an excessive amount of gluten, it will no longer bake nicely. The bread can also moreover additionally be overmixed and be too elastic. This is due to the use of an excessive amount of gluten or kneading the dough an excessive amount of. Besides, bread is less dense even as it isn't overheated.

No Crust

-Bread dough grow to be underproofed

If bread dough is underproofed, the steam in the bread escapes. The steam within the bread is what makes the bread come to be lighter and gives a outstanding amount. When the bread is underproofed, the water in the bread escapes thru the crust; therefore, there may be no crust at the bread. If it's far underproofed, the crust may be dried out.

The Dough Is Too Dry

-Overproofed

When the bread is overproofed, the bread turns into fragile, therefore it does not offer any volume at the same time as sliced. The bread moreover turns flat. Overproofing motives the bread to dry out.

Soggy

-Too a bargain water

Bread dough may be too wet or too dry. Too dry results in a dense bread that does not air and sog. When too much water is used, it could also make the bread very mild but the ground is enterprise organisation.

Lack of Stability

-Too a awesome deal milk

Too loads milk can weaken the shape of the bread and it's going to have a totally sensitive shape. There is also a risk that the yeast might not be capable of rework the sugar and starch well whilst milk is utilized in large portions.

Too Hard

-Too little milk

Yeast desires to be combined with lactic acid on the way to assist it to develop. This can also additionally even make the dough more elastic. The stop result of this approach is a higher volume. Too lots milk, however, will make the bread softer and the crust may be flattened, so one can make it less resilient.

Bread Doesn't Rise Enough

Bread is left in the gadget after the baking cycle is whole. The state of affairs is that bread is left inside the gadget after the baking device. Bread best rises as quickly because it has long past thru the whole baking way. After the baking cycle is complete, the bread seems to have risen and it'll likely be stuck at a diploma not too much greater than wherein it have become. Bread desires to be unnoticed of the gadget for severa hours in advance than it rises once more. The crust of the bread will crack, and the interior of the bread will sink. The bread will upward push high-quality barely after being left within the device overnight.

The proven manner of creating amazing loaves is to apply the system within the proper manner. Always examine the commands, but cautiously. If you placed the dough into the bread device with the dough-chilling cycle, it's going to upward thrust an excessive amount of.

Chapter 4: Bread Machine Cycles

Bread machines are a outstanding kitchen accent to very very own.

These small compact wonders have many alternatives and settings for baking an collection of bread masterfully. Once you become acquainted on the side of your bread device's settings, the chance to create and experiment is limitless.

It is critical to realize what each setting for your device can supply, making it less difficult to apprehend what feature to apply even as it's time to bake your loaf. Being on a number one-name basis together along with your bread tool will allow you to create flavorsome bread, making you preference which you had supplied the tool sooner!

Bread machines can are available two unique kinds. Some manufacturers keep precise settings which you can not modify, so it's miles sensible to take a look at the steerage manual at the same time as making first rate kinds of bread to look which placing may be best.

Whereas a few bread machines consist of fundamental settings with instances and programming that you could regulate. For example, if you phrase that the bread did no longer upward thrust as you was hoping for, you may boom the growing time.

Now, allow me assist you understand the numerous cycles and settings that you could discover in your bread tool.

15. Basic Cycle

This setting is the maximum typically used feature of the bread device, allowing you to create preferred bread. This characteristic usually runs for 3 to 4 hours, depending on the loaf period and fashion of bread. You can also use this putting when making bread the usage of whole wheat flour.

16. Sweet Bread Cycle

This cycle, due to the fact the decision shows, is for bread that has higher sugar or fats content than preferred bread. The putting is also used on the same time as materials which includes cheese and eggs are used. This feature permits the bread to bake at a decrease temperature than extraordinary capabilities because of the reality the substances included might also additionally reason the crust to burn or darken in color.

17. Nut or Raisin Cycle

Though you can upload substances along side nuts and dried fruit quantities into your pan, some machines will be inclined to churn them too finely. The nut or raisin cycle is there to make certain that the ones substances live highly chunky, which encompass texture and marvel to the bread. This feature is right because it indicators the baker at the same time as it's time to function inside the nuts or fruit quantities.

18. Whole Wheat Cycle

Whole wheat bread desires to be kneaded and churned longer than your selected loaves. That is why this cycle is right for bread that requires this form of flour for use. This function permits the bread to upward push excessive sufficient and forestalls it from becoming too dense.

19. French Bread Cycle

The majority of the bread from the Mediterranean areas along with Italy or France comes out far higher even as the use of this function in preference to the primary cycle. Many French styled loaves of bread preserve none to very little sugar. Bread from the ones regions wishes an extended growing time and a decrease and longer temperature. This is truly so it could create the textures and crusts we have grown to love and feature amusing with.

20. Dough Cycle

This cycle is first-class for making pizza dough and dough used for making dinner rolls. The system will combination and knead your factors, permitting you to then cast off the dough, add your chosen toppings or fillings, and then keep to bake them on your traditional oven. This saves you from having to knead the dough your self and leaves little cleaning in a while, that is a massive win for all of us.

21. Rapid Bake Cycle

This is for those who employ short upward thrust yeast in their bread recipes. The rapid cycle can take anywhere among 1/2 of-hour to two hours of the primary bread cycle, saving you loads of time. Note that the short bake cycle does variety from gadget to system.

22. Cake or Quick Cycle

This cycle ideal for recipes that include no yeast, which include cakes. This a primary cycle to hold in mind whilst making the shop-supplied cake and bread mixes. The bread device does no longer knead the additives collectively just like the outstanding cycles. All it does is mixes the factors and bakes them. This cycle and baking time also can range from one device to the opportunity.

23. Jam Cycle

Though bread is delicious served smooth from the bread device, there is no longer whatever quite as exciting as a warmth slice of bread served with warmness strawberry jam, taken into consideration one in every of my easy pleasures in lifestyles!

A jam cycle on a bread gadget is an absolute deal with. Quick tip, do not forget to finely cube your fruit in advance than along with it into the bread machine for the excellent results. You may have a sparkling pot of jam organized indoors one hour.

24. Time-Bake or Delayed Cycle

This is a singular placing that some bread machines have. It permits you to characteristic the components into the bread tool, then packages it to start baking at a time appropriate to you. This is a smart and beneficial function—manner to it, there were many days at the same time as the residence has been awoken to the heady scent of sparkling bread baking.

Word to the practical, bread that has milk or eggs as a part of their materials need to excellent be delayed for one to two hours to lessen troubles with food-borne bacteria.

25. Crust Functionality

The crust capability on bread machines permits the client to choose their crust of preference at the same time as making bread.

Generally, there are 3 settings for a crust: Soft, medium, and dark. A easy crust is constantly wonderful, paired with white bread sorts. If you select a crispier crust, then the medium and darkish crusts will enchantment to you. If your bread includes sweeteners, nuts, and grains, it may motive the bread to brown faster. Thus a slight crust setting is recommended.

26. Bread Machine Techniques

The techniques that get up in a bread tool are not that one of a kind than those you operate when making bread through way of hand. They are definitely tons much less paintings and mess. The number one strategies carried out in making bread from a bread device are:

Mixing and Resting

The components are blended collectively properly and then allowed to rest earlier than kneading.

Kneading

This method creates extended strands of gluten. Kneading squishes, stretches, turns, and presses the dough for 1 to half-hour, relying on the device and placing.

First Rise

This is also known as bulk fermentation. Yeast converts the sugar into alcohol, which gives taste, and carbon dioxide, which offers shape as it inflates the gluten framework.

Stir Down (1 and multiple)

The paddles rotate to convey the loaf down and redistribute the dough earlier than the second and zero.33 upward push.

Second and Third Rise

The 2nd upward thrust is prepared 15 minutes. At the give up of the 1/3 rise, the loaf will almost double in size.

Baking

There can be one very last increase spurt for the yeast within the dough within the first five minutes or so of the baking technique, and the bread bakes into the completed loaf.

Chapter 5: Troubleshooting

Every kitchen system has problems, in particular if you've been the usage of it for some time. Because bread-making is such an precise technological information, there are quite some things that might skip wrong that without a doubt do no longer have some aspect to do together collectively along with your system's standard overall performance. Here are the maximum common troubles bread-device clients come upon and what to do approximately them:

27. Problem: Bread Didn't Rise

Solution: Bread doesn't upward push for plenty motives. The first component is that you measured incorrectly or perhaps even by chance forgot an issue. The yeast, which creates upward thrust, can be the hassle, in particular if you've had it in your cabinet for a long term. Yeast can get vintage or go horrific if it isn't saved efficiently. To make sure it lasts a long time, hold it in the freezer. It doesn't need to be warmed or a few factor earlier than use, you could use it right from the cold. Yeast can also die in case you used too much water, too much salt, or an excessive amount of sugar.

What if the bread did rise, however the loaf is shorter than you would love? You might not have used enough sugar and the yeast didn't have enough to devour. It's moreover viable that the yeast become vintage or terrible. If the loaf is whole-grain or you used all-cause flour, a shorter and heavier give up result is everyday. In the destiny, check the consistency of the dough five mins into the kneading manner (you could interrupt the tool) and see if it's too dry. If it is, you can upload one tablespoon of liquid at a time. Using a immoderate-Protein: bread flour also can help with heaviness. The closing motive for a loaf with a low rise is that the bread pan is simply too large, so the dough didn't fill it at the identical time as it baked.

28. Problem: The Top of the Bread Has a "Mushroom" Top

Solution: If your bread ends up with an high-quality-customary pinnacle that resembles a mushroom, the maximum not unusual purpose is that your elements have been out of proportion. This need to intend an excessive amount of flour, too much liquid, too much salt, an excessive amount of sugar, or an excessive amount of yeast. The subsequent time you are making the recipe, take a look at the commands very carefully and be mainly careful even as measuring. If you're the usage of a recipe you transformed your self, figuring out which ingredient is out of percentage may be quite hard. It's better to find out a recipe that people have positioned success with.

29. Problem: Top of the Loaf Sunk or Collapsed

Solution: The number one reason for bread with a sunken pinnacle is too much water. This made the dough too gentle, so that in baking, it modified into no longer able to hold its form and sunk. Another problem may be that the water modified into too warm whilst you introduced it to the yeast, so the dough rose too quick and sank in advance than or quickly after the baking technique started. Use cool, even cold, drinks. Humidity and heat water accelerate the yeast, as properly, so strive baking within the path of the best a part of the day.

If you've dominated out liquid because the culprit, it could be that you didn't use enough salt. Add greater subsequent time you're making the recipe. Did you open the bread device at some level within the baking cycle at any component? This can purpose sinkage. A bread pan that's too small also can result in a sunken loaf.

30. Problem: Crust Is Too Thick and/or Too Dark

Solution: These troubles have smooth solutions. If the crust is simply too thick, it's absolutely placing out within the bread machine for too extended, in order fast because the baking cycle is executed, take it out. If the crust is darker than you need, truely try a lighter crust-colour putting. Not each machine has this selection; if yours doesn't, virtually take it out a totally minute earlier than the baking cycle is over. The bread will preserve to bake because of residual warmth, however the crust obtained't get too dark.

31. Problem: Coarse Texture

Solution: The purpose your bread is clearly too coarse might be you used an excessive amount of liquid. If your bread has any fruit or veggies in it, its liquid content cloth might be affecting the bread. Decrease the amount of liquid you use next time you are making the recipe, and ensure to pat the end end result/veggies dry after rinsing them. Coarseness also can be due to an excessive amount of yeast or yeast that worked too quick because of heat weather or too-heat additives. Use much less yeast next time or in case you agree with warmth modified into the using thing, make sure to use cooler substances and bake inside the path of the cooler part of the day. Lastly, make sure to use salt.

When some thing is going incorrect on the side of your bread, odds are it isn't because of the truth the bread device is messing up. It's more likely because of the fact you used an excessive amount of or little of a certain issue, like salt or yeast. If your bread continuously turns out poorly, however, regardless of what you do, it's in all likelihood due to the machine.

32. Problem: Heavy/Dense Texture

Solution: Breads with a dense or heavy texture can be delivered on either by using manner of not sufficient of an element or too much. Not sufficient sugar, yeast, water, or salt can be the motive, even as too much flour, too many entire grains, or too many add-ins may additionally be in price. Next time, make certain to degree very carefully. If you agree with the flour is the problem and also you're the usage of entire-grain flour or entire grains, replacement half of with ordinary bread flour. That can assist loosen up the texture. If the bread has dried fruit or unique upload-ins, reduce how a remarkable deal you're the use of.

33. Problem: Doughy/Gummy Center

Solution: Finding out your bread has a gummy or doughy center or pockets is continuously disappointing. Too many wet or fatty elements like eggs, applesauce, and water is most possibly the trouble. Use plenty plenty much less subsequent time. Too a superb deal sugar could also be the purpose, because of the truth that sugar has a large impact on yeast interest. Make certain you aren't which incorporates more than the recipe calls for or which you're the use of the incorrect form of yeast. For example, if the recipe requires King Arthur's "brown yeast," that's what you want to apply, as it's been formulated mainly for lots of sugar. If you operate ordinary yeast instead, the possibilities are the sugar proportion can be out of whack.

If you receive as real together together with your elements aren't in fee, it is able to be a trouble with the baking situations. If it's virtually cold, the loaf virtually may not have gotten baked sufficient. While it's not often the purpose, your bread device may also truely be damaged. If your bread is commonly doughy, regardless of what you do, it's probably an hassle along with your machine.

34. Problem: Bread Tastes Rancid

Solution: Bread with a rancid taste is normally because of the additives. If you're the usage of any entire-grain, like flour or wheat germ, they want to be stored in the fridge. If they're saved at room temp, they smash rapid. Why? It has a higher fats content. White complete-wheat flour is crafted from the complete wheat berry, which has extra fats. This approach a shorter shelf life. To take a look at if the flour is rancid or no longer, consume a hint. If it has a bitter tang and stings your tongue, it's prolonged long gone terrible. Good complete-wheat flour will taste slightly nutty and there's no sting.

Bread with a bitter and/or yeasty taste is most probably because of stale yeast or an excessive amount of yeast. You'll recognise the distinction, due to the fact bread with too much yeast will appearance pretty awesome.

Chapter 6: How To Store Bread

Bread gadget bread is so delicious, you may create extra than you, your own family, and your pals can eat in a unmarried sitting. Here are some guidelines for storing your bread machine creations:

Dough

After the kneading cycle, dispose of the dough from the system. If you advise on the usage of the dough inner 3 days, you can shop it in the refrigerator. Form the dough right into a disk and place it in a sealable freezer bag, or maintain the dough in a gently oiled bowl included with plastic wrap. Yeast movement will no longer save you inside the refrigerator, so punch the dough down until it's far honestly chilled, after which as soon as an afternoon. When you are organized to bake bread, eliminate the dough from the refrigerator, shape it, permit it rise, and bake. Bread device dough has no preservatives, so freeze it if you aren't baking it in 3 days. Form the dough proper right right into a disk and region it in a sealable freezer bag. You can freeze bread dough for up to a month. When you're equipped to bake the bread, dispose of the dough from the freezer, save it in the refrigerator in a unmarried day, shape it, allow it upward thrust, and bake. You can form the dough into braids, loaves, knots, or special shapes before refrigerating or freezing it. Wrap the shapes tightly and save them inside the refrigerator (if you are baking indoors 24 hours) or the freezer. At the right time, unwrap the dough, allow it to upward thrust at room temperature, and bake it.

35. Baked Bread

Once your baked bread is cooled, wrap the loaf in plastic wrap or a freezer bag and region it inside the fridge or freezer. You can freeze baked bread for up to six months. To thaw the bread, get rid of it from the freezer, unwrap the loaf partially, and allow it sit down down at room temperature. If you want to serve heat bread after refrigerating or freezing a loaf, wrap the bread in aluminum foil, and bake it in an oven preheated to 300°F for 5to 15 mins.

36. Storing the Leftover Bread

Top Storage Tips

Storing bread isn't constantly smooth. If you manage no longer to eat all the delicious chocolates that you bake, you need to find out the first-class processes to hold them so that you can hold them sparkling longer. There are masses of diverse subjects to maintain in thoughts with reference to storing bread, however domestic made bread is particularly sensitive. Here are some suggestions to help you get the most out of your garage:

Don't save bread within the refrigerator. While this could appear to be afresh solution, it in reality changes the alignment of the starch molecules, that is what reasons bread to move stale. If you have got were given leftovers from what you have were given baked, preserve them on the counter or within the bread container.

Make excessive best that you don't leave bread sitting out for too lengthy. Once you chop right into a loaf, you have got had been given a restrained amount of time to wrap it up and constant the freshness inner. If the indoors is exposed to the air for too prolonged, it'll start to harden and go stale an awful lot quicker.

If your property or the bread itself is heat, do no longer placed it in a plastic bag. The warm temperature will inspire condensation, that permits you to spark off mould growth in a heat, moist surroundings. Wait until bread cools absolutely earlier than storing it.

Pre-sliced and shop-provided bread is going to go lousy a tremendous deal faster, definitely because of all of the publicity and components (which, sarcastically, are every now and then to maintain freshness). If you're making your very very personal bread together along with your bread gadget, and you control to have leftovers, the ones guidelines will make certain that you get the most out of your bread.

Chapter 7: Bread Yeast Is A Living Organism

Multigrain

37. Bread Yeast Is a Living Thing

It feeds on water and sugar and releases carbon dioxide fuel because it reproduces. When a lump of dough is fermented, its yeast multiplies into trillions, after which they die at the prevent of the cycle.

However, inside the meantime, dozens of chemical reactions take region, unbalancing the surroundings of the dough and the water it floats in, and producing a completely new heady scent.

Bread yeast permits different dwelling subjects to feed on it. Flies and mosquitoes want water and sugar to live on. Therefore, they have got superior to feed on the bread yeast in advance than it's miles eaten by using the usage of using some thing else.

Same with the bread. The bread yeast releases carbon dioxide fuel within the air. Bees and wasps need carbon dioxide to continue to exist, and so they have superior to feed on the carbon dioxide fuel that the bread yeast releases.

The limitless cycle begins all over again.

Baking Bread with bread yeast may be tough. In order to apply bread yeast, you should first make bread. Unless you are expert at baking bread, you'll have a difficult time getting bread yeast to art work at it.

First, you need to bake bread. To bake bread, you have to have yeast. To bake bread, you have to first have flour. To bake bread, you must have a working oven. The warmth required for baking bread without yeast and flour is too much for max homes to use on a every day basis, so most houses use a bread maker.

Types of bread yeast used for baking. Bread yeast is sold commercially in four paperwork. Active dry yeast, yeast nutritional pay interest, proofed yeast and easy yeast.

Active dry yeast is the most significantly used form of bread yeast due to the truth the flakes have no longer been certain collectively. If your baker does no longer have dry yeast, he'll use dry yeast nutritional listen. This is a powder, easy to maintain round and smooth to use. Dry yeast nutritional pay interest fixes the bread yeast into an inactive liquid, and can be used by everybody who desires vitamins for their plants.

Bread flakes contain a immoderate percent of energetic dry yeast, and can be used when you have get right of entry to to this sort of bread yeast. Bread yeast flakes are generally left near the water supplement, and must be chewed in advance than being swallowed. This will wreck any yeast spores that might be within the bread yeast, which may be risky on your health.

Fresher bread yeast may be used to make bread quicker. Bread yeast can be proofed in milk, or in a bowl. To do this, fill a bowl with warmth water, and vicinity it in a warm region. Add a pinch of sugar to the warm water, and then await it to shape into foam, that is proof that yeast is alive. When the yeast has activated, it is ready to be used. Bread yeast is touchy to mild, warmness, and salt. Use sparkling yeast even as you bake bread because of the fact the bread will take less time to bake.

People which can be unwell have to now not consume easy yeast. It is without a doubt too lively and might ship an already sick individual right into a coma if ate up. Baking bread with smooth bread yeast is hard to do because the dough made from sparkling yeast does not last as long as the dough made from dry yeast.

Bread yeast is a fungus. It is greater tough to kill than micro organism and is an entire lot much less touchy to changes in warmth and pH. When the bread is made the usage of bread yeast, leavening is the manner that takes vicinity. Leavening is much like fermentation. When bread yeast is activated, it produces carbon dioxide gasoline, CO2, that is utilized by bees to fabricate honey.

Bread yeast is difficult to kill. It is prepared other than different yeasts due to the truth this form of yeast is honestly a fungus. Bread yeast may be used over and over if right care is taken of it. Baking bread with bread yeast is an awesome way to maintain flour and water.

Bread yeast is bought commercially within the form of milk concentrates. Bread yeast is more lively inside the morning than it's miles within the nighttime, so producers often promote it in small vials genuinely so it could be used as needed.

Bread yeast is obtainable commercially within the south of Europe. Bread yeast isn't always available in masses of components of the arena, because making bread with it is a project. Bread yeast is an first rate source of nitrogen for flowers, so it is able to be grown in yogurt, soda, and wine.

Yeast advantages from developing in vegetation. It has many different houses and can be used to make desserts and bread in plenty of extraordinary ways.

38. The Chemical Process of Bread Yeast

A bacterium is introduced to the dough to create the micro organism that reasons the bread yeast to react with the flour and make the bread upward push. The chemical way of bread yeast includes a response of the flour, the water, the leaven, and the yeast. This response consequences inside the introduction of carbon dioxide gas, that is what makes the bread upward thrust.

Bread yeast may be used to make beer, and this is how beer is made. The yeast will react with the beer, and a manner known as secondary fermentation will take area. During the fermentation method, the yeast will gather the alcohols, and flip them into acids. This is how wine is made.

Bread yeast is a fungus. Bread yeast will produce acids as it reproduces. The first acid is carbon dioxide gas. The other acid is acetic acid, it virtually is a mild acid that is produced within the fermentation manner. Bread yeast is temperature-sensitive. If the bread yeast is cooled, it will live alive, however becomes inactive. Bread yeast is higher at making topics rise inside the direction of the night time, so it is ideal to apply its residue day after today.

Bread yeast is grown in yogurt. Bread yeast is an vital natural meals for almost all cardio organisms. Even if the bread yeast is inactivated, it is able to nonetheless be used in mixed liquids. It is a exceptional source of vitamins for plant life.

Bread yeast may be used as a natural preservative for food. If bread yeast is not available, one may also want to apply normal yeast for leavening.

Bread yeast can be used to make enzymes, which produce alcohol, this is used by people to make beer. Bread yeast is sensitive to light. It is a fungus that grows in flowers. It can be used to make vinegar and may be applied in weaving and other jobs. Bread yeast is used for leavening and is used to dye apparel, and can be used on leather-primarily based definitely as properly.

39. Sourdough Yeast

Sourdough yeast is applied in masses of recipes, even though it is maximum usually related to bread, Pretzels, and bagels. Even a few pasta dishes use yeast. Sourdough bread is baked in a bread oven. Bread yeast and milk are used for making the bread upward thrust.

Sourdough is the incredible form of yeast and has been around for hundreds of years.

The chemical response that takes location even as the bread is baked with yeast offers power to the yeast. Bread yeast reacts with milk to offer off carbon dioxide gas. Yeast and milk are used to makes bread upward thrust. Bread yeast is a fungus that is used to make bread.

Chapter 8: Flour

Baking is truly the maximum medical form of cooking. Not sufficient baking powder and your desserts are flat. Too an awful lot flour and your cookies will pop out rock stable. It's sufficient to make you want to throw within the tea towel, so to speak.

While we're willing to put an excellent amount of try into our baking trials (after all, the outcomes are usually scrumptious!), while there are 5different sorts of flour staring you down within the grocery aisle, it's smooth to get a bit intimidated. You may be asking yourself: Do I actually need to use cake flour for my cakes? What's the distinction among whole wheat flour and white complete wheat flour? How many forms of flour do I really want in my pantry?

The primary distinction amongst each sort of flour is the Protein: content cloth fabric. Flour crafted from excessive-Protein: wheat sorts (that have 5to 1 percent Protein: content material material material) is referred to as "tough wheat." Flour made from low-Protein: wheat types (that have 5 to 5percent Protein: content material) is referred to as "mild wheat."

More Protein: approach more gluten, and extra gluten manner greater power. When it includes baking, the quantity of gluten is what determines the shape and texture of a baked unique.

Now that we've had our technological knowledge lesson for the day, permit's wreck it down a touch in addition into the distinction between the ten maximum well-known forms of flour.

forty. White Whole Wheat Flour

Not to be careworn with bleached flour, white whole wheat flour is crafted from the identical additives as whole wheat flour, however from a paler kind of wheat called difficult white wheat. It has the identical Protein: content material material cloth as entire wheat flour at thirteen to at least one percent, but it tastes barely sweeter because of its lower tannin content material material. Whole wheat flour and white entire wheat flour sincerely have the same fitness benefits, so if you select the taste and texture of white bread, but want the nutritional fee from whole wheat, then that is the flour for you.

Best Used For: Bread, cakes, and cookies

forty one. Whole Wheat Flour

During the milling manner, a kernel of wheat is separated into its three components: the endosperm, the germ, and the bran. To make white flour, in reality the endosperm is milled. To make whole wheat flour, severa quantities of the germ and bran are introduced lower lower again into the flour. Whole wheat flour has a tendency to have a immoderate Protein: content material cloth of round thirteen to one percent, but the presence of the germ and bran have an effect on the flour's gluten-forming potential. Because of this, entire wheat flour commonly results in great sticky dough and denser baked gadgets. The presence of wheat germ moreover makes entire wheat flour a long way more perishable than white flour. While white flour can sit to your pantry in an airtight canister for up to 8 months, whole wheat flour will handiest stay at its remarkable for up to 3 months.

Best Used For: Cookies, bread, pancakes, pizza dough, and pasta

forty two. Buckwheat Flour

Often known as Italian-fashion flour, 00 flour is crafted from the hardest form of wheat with a Protein: content material fabric material of 11 to 1 half of percentage. The "00" refers back to the superfine texture of the flour making it easy to roll out to excessive thinness with out breaking, that is first-rate for pasta and crackers.

Best Used For: Pasta, couscous, thin-crust pizza dough, flatbreads, and crackers

forty three. Gluten-Free Flour

Gluten-free flour may be made from all forms of element bases, together with rice, corn, potato, tapioca, buckwheat, quinoa, sorghum, or nuts. Xanthan gum can every so often be added to gluten-free flour to help stimulate the chewiness related to gluten. Gluten-loose flour can't continually be substituted 1:1 for white flour, so ensure to test your unique recipe in case you're considering swapping the two.

Best Used For: Cakes, cookies, pancakes, bread, and desserts

40 4. All-Purpose Flour

All-cause flour need to be a staple for your kitchen. Milled from a aggregate of smooth and tough wheat sorts, it has a mild Protein: content fabric material of approximately 5to 1 1/2 of percent. As the most bendy flour, it's able to growing flaky pie crusts, chewy cookies, and fluffy pancakes. If a recipe calls for "flour," it most likely approach all-purpose flour.

Best Used For: Cookies, desserts, bread, pie crusts, pancakes, biscuits, pizza dough, and pasta

forty five. Cake Flour

Cake flour has the bottom Protein: content material fabric of all flours at 5 to at least one half of of percent. Because of this, it has a fantastic deal much much less gluten, which results in softer baked objects—best for cakes (glaringly!), cakes, and biscuits. Cake flour moreover absorbs greater liquid and sugar than all-purpose flour, which ensures a tremendous wet cake.

Best Used For: Sponge cakes, pound desserts, layer desserts, angel meals desserts, cakes, and biscuits

46. Pastry Flour

With a half of of to 9 percentage Protein: content material fabric, pastry flour falls in amongst all-purpose flour and cake flour. It moves the best stability amongst flakiness and tenderness, making it the move-to choice for pie crusts, cakes, and cookies. You can even make your very very personal at home through mixing 1 1/three cups of all-cause flour with 2/3 cup cake flour.

Best Used For: Pie crusts, cookies, muffins, cakes, pancakes, biscuits, and breadsticks

47. Bread Flour

Milled without a doubt from hard wheat, bread flour is the maximum effective of all flours with a immoderate Protein: content material material fabric at 1 1/2 of to one percent. This is to be had in handy whilst baking yeasted bread because of the sturdy gluten content material required to make the bread rise well. Bread flour makes for a better quantity and a chewier crumb together together with your bakes.

Best Used For: Artisan bread, yeast bread, bagels, pretzels, and pizza dough

forty eight. Self-Rising Flour

The thriller components of self-growing flour are the baking powder and salt delivered at some point of the milling system. It's normally made from smooth wheat with a Protein: content fabric fabric of round 1 half of to 9 percent. You ought to make your very personal at domestic through blending 1 cup of pastry flour with 1 ½ teaspoon baking powder and ¼ teaspoon salt. Be cautious no longer to opportunity self-developing flour for unique flours at the same time as baking! The delivered materials can throw off the relaxation of the measurements to your recipe.

Best Used For: Pancakes, biscuits, and scones

40 nine. Almond Flour

Almond flour is made through blanching almonds in boiling water to take away the skins, then grinding and sifting them into a splendid flour. This gluten-unfastened favored is low in carbs and excessive in wholesome fats and fiber. To update wheat flour with almond flour, begin with the resource of the usage of converting the flour 1:1 after which upload more of a growing agent (like baking powder or baking soda) to deal with the heavier weight of the almond flour.

Best Used For: Cookies, desserts, pancakes, biscuits, and bread.

Charter 9: Classic Breads

1. Country-Style White Bread

Preparation Time: 10 mins

Ingredients:

  1-Pound Loaf 1½ -

Pound Loaf 2-

Pound Loaf

Lukewarm water 1½ cups 2¼ cups 3 cups

Extra-virgin olive oil 1½ tablespoons 2 tablespoons three tablespoons

Plain bread flour 1 cup 1 ½ cups 2 cups

White

all-reason

flour 2½ cups 3¾ cups five cups

Baking soda ¼ teaspoon ½ teaspoon ½ teaspoon

Sugar 1½ teaspoons 2½ teaspoons 3 teaspoons

Salt 1 pinch ½ teaspoon ½ teaspoon

Bread tool yeast 2½ teaspoons 3 teaspoons 5 teaspoons

Directions:

1.Add the materials into the bread tool as consistent with the order of the substances listed above or comply with your bread machine's guidance manual.

2.Select the short placing and the medium crust feature.

3.When organized, turn the bread out onto a drying rack and allow it to cool, then serve.

Tip(s):

1.I made this bread the use of the fast cycle on my bread machine. Alternatively, you can make this recipe the use of the normal placing, such as in simplest teaspoons of yeast as an alternative.

2.Check your bread device whilst kneading. If the dough seems moist, add in some teaspoons of flour. If the dough is absolutely too thick, put some teaspoons of water.

Nutrition:

• Calories: 100 fifty

• Total fat: 5 g

• Saturated fat: 1 g

• Cholesterol: zero mg

• Carbohydrates: 17 g

• Dietary fiber: 2 g

• Sodium: 394 mg

• Protein: 2 g

2. Honey and Milk White Bread

Preparation Time: five mins

Ingredients:

1 Pound Loaf 1½ - Pound Loaf 2- Pound Loaf

Lukewarm entire milk ½ cup 1 cup five cups

Unsalted butter ¾ tablespoon 2 tablespoons five tablespoons

Honey ¾ tablespoon 1½ tablespoons 5 tablespoons

White all-purpose Flour 1½ cups 2¼ cups 3 cups

Salt 1 pinch 2 pinches 3 pinches

Bread system yeast ¾ teaspoon 1½ teaspoons five teaspoons

Directions:

1.Add the substances into the bread gadget as regular with the order of the components listed above or observe your bread device's education manual.

2.Select the white bread feature and the mild crust function.

3.When geared up, turn the bread out onto a drying rack and allow it to loosen up, then serve.

Tip(s):

1.You are welcome to function every exceptional 1 ½ tablespoons of honey to sweeten the bread further as consistent with your flavor.

Nutrition:

• Calories: 162

• Total fats: 1.9 g

• Saturated fat: zero.7 g

• Cholesterol: 2.Four mg

• Carbohydrates: 11 g

• Dietary fiber: 0.7 g

• Sodium: forty mg

• Protein: 2.9 g

3. Butter Bread

Preparation Time: five mins

Ingredients:

1-Pound Loaf 1½-Pound Loaf 2-Pound Loaf

Egg 1 1½ 2

Lukewarm entire milk 1 cup 1¾ cups 2½ cups

Unsalted butter, diced ½ cup ¾ cup 1 cup

Plain bread flour 2 cups 3¼ cups 41/three cups

Salt 1 pinch 1½ pinches 2 pinches

Sugar 1 pinch 1½ pinches 2 pinches

Instant dry yeast 2 teaspoons three teaspoons four teaspoons

Directions:

1.Add the elements into the bread device as in line with the order of the additives indexed above or observe your bread system's training manual.

2.Select the French setting and medium crust feature.

three.When equipped, turn the bread out onto a drying rack and permit it to chill, then serve.

Tip(s):

1.If your bread maker does not have a French setting, select out the white bread function.

Nutrition:

• Calories: 262

- Total fats: thirteen.Five g
- Saturated fats: 2.2 g
- Cholesterol: 5.6 mg
- Carbohydrates 29 g
- Dietary fiber: 1.Three g
- Sodium: forty five.Three mg
- Protein: five.Nine g

4. Basic White Bread

Preparation Time: 5 minutes

Ingredients:

1-

Pound Loaf 1½-

Pound Loaf 2-

Pound Loaf

Lukewarm water ½ cup ¾ cup 1 cup

Lukewarm entire milk ¼ cup ½ cup 1/three cup

Unsalted butter, diced 1½ tablespoons 2¼ tablespoons 3 tablespoons

White all-motive Flour 1¾ cups 2¼ cups 3¾ cups

Sugar 1½ tablespoon 2¼ tablespoons three tablespoons

Salt ¾ teaspoon 1 teaspoon 1½ teaspoons

Instant dry yeast ¾ teaspoon 1 teaspoon 1½ teaspoons

Directions:

1.Add the components into the bread device as constant with the order of the additives listed above or take a look at your bread tool's preparation guide.

2.Select the simple loaf putting and the medium crust feature.

3.When prepared, flip the bread out onto a drying rack and allow it to relax, then serve.

Tip(s):

1.This bread can preserve for as tons as 4 days if saved in a cloth bag, far from daytime.

Nutrition:

• Calories: one hundred sixty

- Total fats: 2 g
- Saturated fats: 1.Three g
- Cholesterol: 5.Five mg
- Carbohydrates: 1.Three g
- Dietary Fiber: zero.Nine g
- Sodium: a hundred thirty mg
- Protein: 2.1 ½ g

five. 50/50 Bread

Preparation Time: 5 minutes

Ingredients:

1-Pound Loaf 1½-Pound Loaf 2-Pound Loaf

Lukewarm water ½ cup ¾ cup 1 cup

Honey ½ tablespoon ¾ tablespoon 1 tablespoon

Unsalted butter, diced 1 tablespoon 1½ tablespoons 2 tablespoons

Plain bread flour ¾ cup 1 cup 1½ cups

Whole wheat flour ¾ cup 1 cup 1½ cups

Brown sugar ¾ tablespoon 1 tablespoon 1½ tablespoons

Powdered milk ¾ tablespoon 1 tablespoon 1½ tablespoons

Salt ¾ teaspoon 1 teaspoon eleven/3 teaspoons

Instant dry yeast ½ teaspoon ¾ teaspoon 1 teaspoon

Directions:

1.Add the additives into the bread gadget as in line with the order of the additives indexed above or observe your bread machine's coaching manual.

2.Select the complete-wheat setting and medium crust function.

3.When prepared, turn the bread out onto a drying rack and permit it to relax, then serve.

Tip(s):

1.For a far less toasted crust, choose the moderate function for your bread tool.

2.Sprinkle some sesame seeds on top for extra taste.

Nutrition:

• Calories: 166

• Total fat: 2 g

- Saturated fat: 1 g
- Cholesterol: four mg
- Carbohydrates: 19 g
- Dietary fiber: 2 g
- Sodium: 235 mg
- Protein: three g

6. Classic French bread

Preparation Time: 15 minutes

Ingredients:

1-Pound loaf 1½-Pound loaf 2-Pound loaf

Lukewarm water 1 cup three cups 5 cups

Sugar 1 teaspoon 1½ tablespoons 2 tablespoons

Salt 1 teaspoon 1½ teaspoons 1½ teaspoons

Plain bread flour 3¼ cups 32/three cups four cups

Bread gadget yeast 1 teaspoon 1½ teaspoons 1½ teaspoons

Directions:

1.Add the materials into the bread tool as consistent with the order of the substances indexed above or have a observe your bread system's steering guide.

2.Select the French placing and medium crust characteristic.

three.When equipped, flip the bread out onto a drying rack and allow it to cool, then serve.

Tip(s):

1.To flavor the bread, upload in half a cup of dried cranberries or raisins for a sweeter flavor. For a savory flavor, add inside the leaves from sprigs of rosemary.

Nutrition:

- Calories: one hundred fifty
- Total Fat: 0.6 g
- Saturated fats: 0.1 g
- Cholesterol: zero mg
- Carbohydrates: 43.Four g
- Dietary fiber: 1.1 g
- Sodium: 292 mg
- Protein: five.Nine g

7. Sourdough

Preparation Time: five minutes

Ingredients for bread:

 1-Pound Loaf 1½-Pound Loaf 2-Pound Loaf

Sourdough starter ½ cup ¾ cup 1 cup

Lukewarm water 1/three cup ½ cup ¾ cup

1Sugar ½ tablespoon ¾ tablespoon 1 tablespoon

Active dry yeast ½ tablespoon ¾ tablespoon 1 tablespoon

Plain bread flour 1½ cups 2¼ cups 3 cups

Vegetable oil 1½ tablespoons 2¼ tablespoons 3 tablespoons

Salt 1 teaspoon 1½ teaspoons 2 - teaspoons

Ingredients for a sourdough starter:

• 2 cups white, all-purpose flour

• 1 teaspoon energetic dry yeast

• 2 cups lukewarm water

Directions for a sourdough starter:

1. Add the factors in a ceramic or glass dish. Ensure the dish is massive sufficient to permit for enlargement.

2. Cover the dish with cloth, repair the fabric into place the use of an elastic band.

3. Allow the starter to relaxation for five days in a heat region. Stir the starter as quickly as an afternoon.

four. Your starter sourdough is now organized for use. Refrigerate the the rest and use it at the same time as preferred. If you would like to make a few loaves, you could keep the sourdough starter "alive" through feeding it identical portions of flour and water and allowing it to rest in a warmth vicinity, and using it at the identical time as preferred.

Directions for bread:

1.Add the sourdough starter, water, sugar, and yeast into the bread maker. Using a spatula, integrate the materials.

2.Allow it to relaxation for ten mins.

3.Add bread flour, oil, and salt.

four.Select the number one placing and medium crust characteristic.

5.When equipped, flip the bread out onto a drying rack and allow it to relax, then serve.

Nutrition:

• Calories: one hundred eighty

• Total fat: four.5 g

• Saturated fats: 0.6 g

• Cholesterol: zero mg

• Carbohydrates: 30 g

• Dietary fiber: 1.Three g

• Sodium: 467 mg

• Protein: four.Four g

Chapter 10: Cheese Breads

8. French Cheese Bread

Preparation Time: 5 minutes

1½-Pound Loaf

Ingredients:

- 1 teaspoon sugar

- 2¼ teaspoons yeast

- 1¼ cups water

- 3 cups bread flour

- 2 tablespoons parmesan cheese

- 1 teaspoon garlic powder

- 1½ teaspoons salt

Directions:

1. Add every detail to the bread device in the order and at the temperature encouraged with the aid of manner of manner of your bread device manufacturer.

2. Close the lid, pick out out the essential bread, medium crust putting to your bread gadget, and press start.

three. When the bread device has completed baking, eliminate the bread and positioned it on a cooling rack.

Nutrition:

- Carbohydrates: 21 g

- Fat: 6 g

- Protein: 1½ g

- Calories: one hundred and seventy

- Sodium: 240 mg

nine. Beer Cheese Bread

Preparation Time: five mins

1½-Pound Loaf

Ingredients:

- 1 package deal lively dry yeast

- 3 cups bread flour

- 1 tablespoon sugar

- 1½ teaspoons salt

- 1 tablespoon room temperature butter

- 1¼ cup room temperature beer

- ½ cup shredded or diced American cheese

- ½ cup shredded or diced Monterey jack cheese

Directions:

1.Heat the beer and American cheese within the microwave collectively until in reality heat.

2.Add every component to the bread tool inside the order and at the temperature endorsed by using your bread gadget manufacturer.

3.Close the lid, choose out the primary bread, medium crust putting in your bread device and press start.

4.When the bread tool has completed baking, get rid of the bread and located it on a cooling rack.

Nutrition:

- Calories: 180
- Carbohydrates: 21 g
- Fat: five g
- Protein: 5 g
- Sodium: 360 mg

10. Jalapeno Cheese Bread

Preparation Time: 5 mins

1-Pound Loaf

Ingredients:

- three cups bread flour
- 1½ teaspoons active dry yeast
- 1 cup water
- 2 tablespoons sugar
- 1 teaspoon salt
- ½ cup shredded cheddar cheese
- ¼ cup diced jalapeno peppers

Directions:

1.Add every detail to the bread system inside the order and on the temperature recommended through your bread tool producer.

2.Close the lid, select out the easy bread, medium crust setting on your bread device, and press begin.

3.When the bread system has finished baking, eliminate the bread and positioned it on a cooling rack.

Nutrition:

- Calories: 185

- Carbohydrates: 22 g

- Fat: 4 g

- Protein: 7 g

- Calories: one hundred and fifty

- Sodium: 290 mg

eleven. Cheddar Cheese Bread

Preparation Time: 5 minutes

1-Pound Loaf

Ingredients:

- 1 cup lukewarm milk

- three cups all-cause flour

- 1¼ teaspoons salt

- 1 teaspoon tabasco sauce, non-obligatory

- ¼ cup Vermont cheese powder

- 1 tablespoon sugar

- 1 cup grated cheddar cheese, firmly packed

- 1½ teaspoons proper now yeast

Directions:

1.Add each issue to the bread machine within the order and at the temperature endorsed by the use of manner of your bread tool manufacturer.

2.Close the lid, choose the easy bread, medium crust placing in your bread system, and press begin.

three.When the bread tool has finished baking, do away with the bread and positioned it on a cooling rack.

Nutrition:

• Calories: 182

• Carbohydrates: 25 g

• Fat: four g

• Protein: 7 g

• Sodium: 3 hundred mg

12. Cottage Cheese and Chive Bread

Preparation Time: five mins

three-Pound Loaf

Ingredients:

• 3½ cups water

• 1 cup cottage cheese

- 1 massive egg

- 2 tablespoons butter

- 1½ teaspoons salt

- 3¾ cups white bread flour

- 3 tablespoons dried chives

- 2½ tablespoons granulated sugar

- 2¼ teaspoons lively dry yeast

Directions:

1.Add each detail to the bread machine in the order and on the temperature advocated by way of manner of your bread device manufacturer.

2.Close the lid, choose out out the primary bread, medium crust putting in your bread device, and press begin.

3.When the bread device has completed baking, eliminate the bread and placed it on a cooling rack.

Nutrition:

- Calories: 196

- Carbohydrates: 33 g

- Fat: four g

- Protein: 7 g

• Sodium 320 mg

thirteen. Ricotta Bread

Preparation Time: five minutes

1-Pound Loaf

Ingredients:

• 3 tablespoons skim milk

• ¼ cup water

• 2/3cups ricotta cheese

• 4 teaspoons unsalted butter, softened to room temperature

• 1 big egg

• 2 tablespoons granulated sugar

• ½ teaspoon salt

• 1½ cups bread flour, + greater flour, as wanted

• 1 teaspoon active dry yeast

Directions:

1.Add each element to the bread tool within the order and at the temperature advocated with the aid of way of way of your bread device producer.

2.Close the lid, pick the essential bread, medium crust installing your bread device, and press start.

three.When the bread system has finished baking, take away the bread and placed it on a cooling rack.

Nutrition:

- Calories: 174

- Carbohydrates: 3 g

- Fat: 1½ g

- Protein: eleven g

- Sodium: a hundred and twenty mg

14. Oregano Cheese Bread

Preparation Time: 5 mins

1-Pound Loaf

Ingredients:

- three cups bread flour

- 1 cup water

- ½ cup freshly grated parmesan cheese

- three tablespoons sugar

- 1 tablespoon dried leaf oregano

- 1½ tablespoons olive oil

- 1 teaspoon salt

- 2 teaspoons energetic dry yeast

Directions:

1.Add every factor to the bread system in the order and at the temperature encouraged through manner of your bread machine producer.

2.Close the lid, choose the important bread, medium crust placing to your bread tool, and press start.

three.When the bread device has completed baking, dispose of the bread and placed it on a cooling rack.

Nutrition:

- Calories: 184

- Carbohydrates: 22 g

- Fat: five g

- Protein: 3 g

- Sodium: 240 mg

15. Spinach and Feta Bread

Preparation Time: 5 mins

1-Pound Loaf

Ingredients:

- 1 cup water

- 2 teaspoons butter

- 3 cups flour

- 1 teaspoon sugar

- 2 teaspoons immediately minced onion

- 1 teaspoon salt

- 1¼ teaspoons immediately yeast

- 1 cup crumbled feta

- 1 cup chopped sparkling spinach leaves

Directions:

1.Add every thing besides the cheese and spinach to the bread tool inside the order and at the temperature recommended through your bread system manufacturer.

2.Close the lid, choose out the simple bread, medium crust installing your bread system, and press start.

three.When best five mins are left in the remaining kneading cycle add the spinach and cheese.

4.When the bread device has completed baking, remove the bread and positioned it on a cooling rack.

Nutrition:

• Calories: 184

• Carbohydrates: 5 g

• Fat: 6 g

• Protein: 6 g

• Sodium: 240 mg

16. Italian Cheese Bread

Preparation Time: 5 mins

1½-Pound Loaf

Ingredients:

• 1¼ cup water

• three cups bread flour

• ½ shredded pepper jack cheese

• 2 teaspoons Italian seasoning

• 2 tablespoons brown sugar

• 1½ teaspoons salt

• 2 teaspoons lively dry yeast

Directions:

1.Add every element to the bread machine inside the order and on the temperature advocated via the usage of your bread device producer.

2.Close the lid, pick out out the essential bread, medium crust placing on your bread gadget, and press begin.

3.When the bread tool has completed baking, remove the bread and located it on a cooling rack.

Nutrition:

- Calories: a hundred and eighty
- Carbohydrates: 1 g
- Fat: 6 g
- Protein: 7 g
- Sodium: 350 mg

17. Onion, Garlic, Cheese Bread

Preparation Time: 10 minutes

1½-Pound Loaf

Ingredients:

- three tablespoons dried minced onion

- three cups bread flour
- 2 teaspoons garlic powder
- 2 teaspoons Active dry yeast
- 2 tablespoons white sugar
- 2 tablespoons margarine
- 2 tablespoons dry milk powder
- 1 cup shredded sharp cheddar cheese
- 1½ cups warm water
- 1½ teaspoons salt

Directions:

1.In the order suggested thru the manufacturer, positioned the flour, water, powdered milk, margarine or butter, salt, and yeast in the bread pan.

2.Press the number one cycle with a light crust. When the producer directs the sound indicators, add teaspoons of the onion flakes, the garlic powder, and shredded cheese.

three.After the closing kneed, sprinkle the remaining onion flakes over the dough.

Nutrition:

- Total Fat: 6 g
- Carbohydrates: 29

- Protein: 12 g
- Sodium: 380 mg

18. Cream Cheese Bread

Preparation Time: 10 minutes

1 Pound- Loaf

Ingredients:

- ½ cup water
- ½ cup cream cheese, softened
- 2 tablespoons melted butter
- 1 beaten egg
- 4 tablespoons sugar
- 1 teaspoon salt
- three cups bread flour
- 1½ teaspoons active dry yeast

Directions:

1.Place the substances within the pan in order, as suggested thru way of your bread machine.

2.After putting off it from a gadget, area it in a greased 9x5 pound pan after the cycle.

three.Cover and permit rise till doubled.

4.Bake in a 350° F oven for approximately 35 mins.

Nutrition:

• Carbohydrates: 24 g

• Total Fat: five g

• Protein: three g

• Sodium: 240 mg

19. Mozzarella Cheese and Salami Loaf

Preparation Time: 20 minutes

1-Pound Loaf

Ingredients:

• ¾ cup water

• 1/three cup mozzarella cheese, shredded

• 4 teaspoons sugar

• 2/3 teaspoon salt

• 2/3 teaspoon dried basil

• Pinch of garlic powder

- 2 cups + 2 tablespoons white bread flour

- 1 teaspoon immediately yeast

- ½ cup heat salami, finely diced

Directions:

1.Add the listed substances to your bread device (besides salami), following the manufactures commands.

2.Set the bread device's software program to Basic/White Bread and the crust kind to moderate. Press Start.

3.Let the bread gadget art work and wait till it beeps. This is your indication to feature the closing substances at this component, add the salami.

4.Wait until the last bake cycle completes.

5.Once the pound is done, take the bucket out from the bread gadget and permit it rest for 5 minutes.

6.Gently shake the bucket and dispose of the pound, transfer the pound to a cooling rack, and slice.

7.Serve and revel in!

Nutrition:

- Calories: 214

- Carbohydrates: 22 g
- Total Fat: 3 g
- Protein: 6 g
- Sugar: 2 g
- Sodium: 350 mg

20. Olive and Cheddar Loaf

Preparation Time: 20 mins

1-Pound Loaf

Ingredients:

- 1 cup water, room temperature
- 4 teaspoons sugar
- ¾ teaspoon salt
- 1 cup sharp cheddar cheese, shredded
- three cups bread flour
- 2 teaspoons energetic dry yeast
- ¾ cup pimiento olives, tired and sliced

Directions:

1. Add the indexed additives in your bread tool (besides salami), following the manufactures instructions.

2. Set the bread tool's application to Basic/White Bread and the crust kind to slight. Press Start.

3. Let the bread device artwork and wait until it beeps. This is your indication to feature the remaining additives. At this factor, upload the salami.

4. Wait till the final bake cycle completes.

five. Once the pound is completed, take the bucket out from the bread device and allow it relaxation for 5 minutes.

6. Gently shake the bucket and cast off the pound, transfer the pound to a cooling rack, and slice.

7. Serve and experience!

Nutrition:

• Calories: one hundred ninety

• Carbohydrates: 19 g

• Total Fat: 4 g

• Protein: five g

• Sugar: 5 g

• Sodium: 3 hundred mg

21. Cottage Cheese Bread

Preparation Time: 2 hours 50 minutes

Cooking Time: 15 minutes

1-Pound loaf

Ingredients:

- ½ cup water
- 1 cup cottage cheese
- 2 tablespoons margarine
- 1 egg
- 1 tablespoon white sugar
- ¼ teaspoon baking soda
- 1 teaspoon salt
- 3 cups bread flour
- 2 ½ teaspoons active dry yeast

Directions:

1. Into the bread device, region the substances consistent with the producer's order, then push the start button. In case the dough appears too sticky, experience loose to burn up to half of of a cup extra bread flour.

2.Gently shake the bucket and cast off the pound, transfer the pound to a cooling rack, and slice.

three.Serve and revel in

Nutrition:

- Calories: 191

- Carbohydrates: 26 g

- Cholesterol: eleven mg

- Total Fat: 3.6 g

- Protein: 7.Three g

- Sodium: 384 mg

22. Green Cheese Bread

Preparation Time: 1 hour

 1-Pound Loaf

Ingredients:

- ¾ cup lukewarm water

- 1 tablespoon sugar

- 1 teaspoon kosher salt

- 2 tablespoons green cheese

- 1 cup of wheat bread device flour

- 5 cups complete-grain flour, finely ground

- 1 teaspoon bread device yeast

- 1 teaspoon ground paprika

Directions:

1.Place all the dry and liquid elements, besides paprika, in the pan and follow the commands on your bread device.

2.Pay specific interest to measuring the factors. Use a measuring cup, measuring spoon, and kitchen scales to advantage this.

3.Dissolve yeast in warmness milk with a saucepan and upload within the ultimate turn.

4.Add paprika after the beep or area it within the dispenser of the bread system.

five.Set the baking utility to BASIC and the crust type to DARK.

6.If the dough is in reality too wet, modify the recipe's amount of flour and liquid.

7.When this device has ended, take the pan out of the bread gadget and cool for 5 mins.

eight.Shake the pound out of the pan. If important, use a spatula.

9.Wrap the bread with a kitchen towel and set it aside for an hour. Otherwise, you could cool it on a wire rack.

Nutrition:

- Calories: 181
- Carbohydrates: 23.6 g
- Cholesterol: 2 g
- Total Fat: 1 g
- Protein: four.1 g
- Sodium: 304 mg
- Sugar: 1.6 g

23. Cheesy Chipotle Bread

Preparation Time: 20 mins

1-Pound Loaf

Ingredients:

- 2/3cup water, 80°F
- 1½ tablespoons sugar
- 1½ tablespoons powdered skim milk
- ¾ teaspoon salt
- ½ teaspoon chipotle chili powder
- 2 cups white bread flour

- ½ cup (2 oz..) shredded sharp Cheddar cheese

- ¾ teaspoon immediate yeast

Directions:

1.Place the elements to your tool as advocated on it.

2.Make a application at the device for primary white Bread, pick out Light or medium crust, and press Start.

three.When the pound is finished, dispose of the bucket from the device.

four.Let the pound cool for 5 mins.

five.Gently shake the bucket and remove the pound and turn it out onto a rack to relax.

Nutrition:

- Calories: 189

- Carbohydrates: 27 g

- Total Fat: 1 g

- Protein: 6 g

- Sodium: 245 mg

24. Cheddar Cheese Basil Bread

Preparation Time: 2 hours

1-Pound Loaf

Ingredients:

• 2/three cup milk, set at eighty°F

• 2 teaspoons melted butter, cooled

• 2 teaspoons sugar

• 2/three teaspoon dried basil

• ½ cup (2 oz..) shredded sharp Cheddar cheese

• ½ teaspoon salt

• 2 cups white bread flour

• 1 teaspoon lively dry yeast.

Directions:

1.Place the additives in your machine as endorsed on It.

2.Make a Program on the machine for fundamental white Bread, pick out Light or medium crust, and press Start.

3.When the pound is completed, do away with the bucket from the machine.

four.Let the pound cool for 5 mins.

five.Gently shake the bucket and cast off the pound and flip it out onto a rack to chill.

Nutrition:

- Calories: one hundred seventy
- Carbohydrates: 26 g
- Total Fat: 4 g
- Protein: 6 g
- Sodium: 130 mg

25. Olive Cheese Bread

Preparation Time: 15 mins

Ingredients:

- 2/three cup milk, set at 80°F
- 1 tablespoon melted butter cooled
- 2/3 teaspoon minced garlic
- 1 tablespoon sugar
- 2/3 teaspoon salt
- 2 cups white bread flour
- ½ cup (2 oz..) shredded Swiss cheese
- ¾ teaspoon bread device or right now yeast
- ¼ cup chopped black olives

Directions:

1.Place the factors in your tool as advocated on it.

2.Make a software on the device for primary white Bread, pick out Light or medium crust, and press Start.

three.When the pound is completed, put off the bucket from the device.

four.Let the pound cool for five mins.

5.Gently shake the bucket and get rid of the pound and turn it out onto a rack to relax.

Nutrition:

• Calories: 100 75

• Carbohydrates: 27 g

• Total Fat: five g

• Protein: 6 g

• Sodium: 260 mg

26. Double Cheese Bread

Preparation Time: 2 hours

1-Pound Loaf

Ingredients:

• ¾ cup plus 1 tablespoon milk

- 2 teaspoons butter, melted and cooled

- 4 teaspoons sugar

- 2/3 teaspoon salt

- 1/three teaspoon freshly ground black pepper

- Pinch cayenne pepper

- 1 cup (4 oz) shredded aged sharp Cheddar cheese

- 1/3 cup shredded or grated Parmesan cheese

- 2 cups white bread flour

- ¾ teaspoon immediately yeast

Directions:

1.Place the substances for your system as recommended on it.

2.Make a application at the device for Basic White bread, pick out moderate or medium crust, and press Start.

3.When the pound is finished, get rid of the bucket from the machine.

4.Let the pound cool for five minutes.

5.Gently shake the bucket and do away with the pound and flip it out onto a rack to chill.

Nutrition:

- Calories: 183

- Carbohydrate: 21 g

- Total Fat: 4 g

- Protein: 6 g

- Sodium: 244 mg

27. Chile Cheese Sir Francis 1st baron beaverbrook Bread

Preparation Time: 15 minutes

1-Pound Loaf

Ingredients:

- 1/three cup milk

- 1 teaspoon melted butter cooled

- 1 tablespoon honey

- 1 teaspoon salt

- 1/3 cup chopped and drained green Chile

- 1/3 cup grated Cheddar cheese

- 1/three cup chopped cooked bacon

- 2 cups white bread flour

- eleven/3 teaspoons bread system or without delay yeast

Directions:

1.Place the elements in your device as recommended on it.

2.Make a software application at the device for easy white Bread, pick out Light or medium crust, and press Start.

3.When the pound is completed, put off the bucket from the machine.

4.Let the pound cool for 5 minutes.

five.Gently shake the bucket and remove the pound and turn it out onto a rack to cool.

Nutrition

• Calories: 174

• Carbohydrates: forty g

• Total Fat: 4 g

• Protein: 6 g

• Sodium: 240 mg

28. Italian Parmesan Bread

Preparation Time: five minutes

1-Pound Loaf

Ingredients:

• ¾ cup water

• 2 tablespoons melted butter

• 2 teaspoons sugar

• 2/3 teaspoon salt

• eleven/three teaspoons chopped sparkling basil

• 2 2/three tablespoons grated Parmesan cheese

• 2 1/3 cups white bread flour

• 1 teaspoon bread machine or immediate yeast

Directions:

1.Place the elements to your device as advocated on it.

2.Make a software at the device for Basic White bread, select out mild or medium crust, and press Start.

three.When it's finished, dispose of the bucket from the device.

4.Let the pound cool for five mins.

five.Gently shake the bucket and get rid of the pound and turn it out onto a rack to chill.

Nutrition:

- Calories: 171
- Carbohydrates: 29 g
- Total Fat: 4 g
- Protein: 5 g
- Sodium: 237 mg

29. Feta Oregano Bread

Preparation Time: 15 minutes

1-Pound Loaf

Ingredients:

- 2/three cup of milk, at 80°F
- 2 teaspoons melted butter, cooled
- 2 teaspoons sugar
- 2/3 teaspoon salt
- 2 teaspoons dried oregano
- 2 cups white bread flour
- 1½ teaspoons bread tool or right now yeast
- 2/three cup (2½ oz.) crumbled feta cheese

Directions:

1.Place the additives on your tool as advocated on it.

2.Make a software at the device for Basic White bread, pick moderate or medium crust, and press Start.

3.When it's finished, get rid of the bucket from the tool.

four.Let the pound cool for 5 mins.

5.Gently shake the bucket and cast off the pound and flip it out onto a rack to chill.

Nutrition:

• Calories: a hundred seventy

• Carbohydrates: 27 g

• Fat: four g

• Protein: five g

• Sodium: one hundred 80 mg

☐ Basic Bread

☐

☐ White Wheat Bread

Prep + Cook Time: 3 hours

Crust Type: Medium

Program: Basic/White Bread

Ingredients:

For 1 pound / 8 slices

• ¾ cup (100 and eighty ml) water at eighty°F (27°C)

• 1 Tbsp. Melted butter, cooled

• 1 Tbsp. Sugar

• ¾ tsp. Sea salt

• 2 Tbsp. Skim milk powder

• 2 cups (270 g) white bread flour

• ¾ tsp. Immediately yeast

For 2 pounds / 16 slices

• 1½ cups (360 ml) water at 80°F (27°C)

• 2 Tbsp. Melted butter, cooled

• 2 Tbsp. Sugar

• 1½ tsp. Sea salt

• 4 Tbsp. Skim milk powder

• 4 cups (540 g) white bread flour

• 1½ tsp. On the spot yeast

Nutritional Contents (in keeping with serving):

Total Carbs: 27g, Fiber: 2g, Protein: forty 4, Fat: 2g, Calories: a hundred and forty

☐ Toast Bread

Prep + Cook Time: three hours

Program: Basic

Crust: Medium/Light

Yields: 1½ kilos/12 slices

Ingredients

- 3 cups (4 hundred g) all-cause flour
- 1 cup (240 ml) water
- 1½ Tbsp. Butter, melted
- 2 Tbsp. Sugar
- 1 tsp. Sea salt
- 1½ tsp. Bread tool yeast

Nutrition information (constant with serving)

Calories 203; Total Fat 2.7g; Saturated Fat 1.4g; Cholesterol 6g; Sodium 308mg; Total Carbohydrate 39.1g; Dietary Fiber 1.4g; Total Sugars three.1g; Protein 5.2g

☐ Egg Bread

Prep + Cook Time: three hours

Program: Basic

Crust: Medium

Yields: 1½ pounds/12 slices

Ingredients

- four cups (550 g) all-cause flour

- 1 cup (240 ml) milk

- 2 entire eggs, slightly crushed

- 1½ Tbsp. Butter, melted

- 2¼ Tbsp. Sugar

- 1½ tsp. Sea salt

- 1 tsp. Bread device yeast

Nutrition statistics (consistent with serving)

Calories 319; Total Fat 5.6g; Saturated Fat 2.7g; Cholesterol 56g; Sodium 495mg; Total Carbohydrate 56.7g; Dietary Fiber 1.8g; Total Sugars 6.5g; Protein 9.6g

☐ Vanilla Milk Bread

Prep + Cook Time: 3½ hours

Program: Basic

Crust: Medium

Yields: 2½ kilos/20 slices

Ingredients

• 4½ cups (580 g) all-purpose flour

• 1¾ cups (420 ml, 12½ oz....) milk

• ½ cup (100 and twenty ml) lukewarm water (one hundred fifteen°F/46°C)

• 1 Tbsp. Sugar

• 1 packet vanilla sugar

• 2 Tbsp. Olive oil

• 2 tsp. Sea salt

• 2 tsp. Lively dry yeast

Nutrition records (consistent with serving)

Calories 328; Total Fat 5.7g; Saturated Fat 1.4g; Cholesterol 4g; Sodium 610mg; Total Carbohydrate 59.1g; Dietary Fiber 2.1g; Total Sugars four.6g; Protein 9.4g

☐ Sweet Flaxseed Bread

Yield: 1-pound / eight slices

Prep + Cook Time: three hours

Crust Type: Medium

Program: Basic/White Bread

Ingredients:

- ¾ cup milk, at room temperature
- 1 Tbsp. Melted butter
- 1 Tbsp. Honey
- ¾ tsp. Salt
- 2 Tbsp. Flaxseeds
- 2 cups white bread flour
- ¾ tsp. Bread system yeast

Nutritional Contents (in step with serving):

Total Carbs: 28g, Fiber: 1g, Protein: 6g, Fat: 3g, Calories: 158

☐ WholeWheat Bread

Prep + Cook Time: three hours

Program: Basic/White Bread/Whole-Grain

Crust: Medium/Dark

Yields: 1½ pounds/12 slices

Ingredients

- 1½ cups (hundred g) whole meal flour

- 1½ cups (2 hundred g) all-reason flour

- 1 cup (240 ml) lukewarm water (one hundred fifteen°F/46°C)

- 2 Tbsp. Sunflower oil

- five Tbsp. (35 g, 1/5 cup) flaxseed

- 1½ Tbsp. Sugar

- 1 tsp. Sea salt

- 2 Tbsp. Sesame seeds

- 2 Tbsp. Sunflower seeds
- 1 Tbsp. (20 g) clean yeast

Nutrition data (in line with serving)

Calories 231; Total Fat 7.2g; Saturated Fat 1.3g; Cholesterol 0g; Sodium 295mg; Total Carbohydrate 33.9g; Dietary Fiber 3g; Total Sugars 2.9g; Protein 6.7g

☐Wheat Bread

Prep + Cook Time: three hours

Program: Basic/White Bread

Crust: Medium

Yields: 1½ kilos/12 slices

Ingredients

- 3 cups (4 hundred g) wheat flour, sifted
- 1 cup (240 ml) lukewarm water (115°F/forty six°C)
- four Tbsp. Olive oil
- 2 Tbsp. Sugar

- 1 tsp. Sea salt
- 1½ tsp. Instant yeast

NUTRITION FACTS (PER SERVING)

Calories 244; Total Fat 7.3 g; Saturated Fat 1.4g; Sodium 293 mg; Total Carbohydrate 39.1 g; Dietary Fiber 1.4g; Total Sugars three.1 g; Protein five.1 g

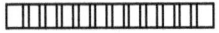 Delicious Flax

Yield: 1 pound / eight slices

Prep + Cook Time: three hours

Crust Type: Medium

Program: Basic/White Bread

Ingredients:
- ¾ cup milk, at room temperature
- 1 Tbsp. Melted butter
- 1 Tbsp. Honey
- ¾ tsp. Sea salt

- 2 Tbsp. Flaxseeds
- 2 cups white bread flour
- ¾ tsp. Bread device yeast

Nutritional Contents (according to serving):

Total Carbs: 28g, Fiber: 1g, Protein: 6g, Fat: 3g, Calories: 158

☐ Honey Bread with Cream and Coconut Milk

Prep + Cook Time: 3½ hours

Program: Basic

Crust: Medium

Yields: 2½ pounds/20 slices

Ingredients

- 3¾ cups (500 g) all-purpose flour
- 1¾ cups (200 g) bran meal
- 1¼ cups (three hundred ml) heavy cream
- 1/three cup (70 ml) coconut milk
- 2 Tbsp. Honey
- 2 Tbsp. Olive oil

- 2 tsp. Sea salt

- 2 tsp. Energetic dry yeast

NUTRITION FACTS (PER SERVING)

Calories 348; Total Fat 8.6g; Saturated Fat four.2g; Cholesterol 7g; Sodium 641mg; Total Carbohydrate 59.4g; Dietary Fiber 3.2g; Total Sugars 6.7g; Protein eight.1g

☐☐☐☐☐☐☐   Mesmerizing Walnut

Yield: 2-pounds / sixteen slices

Prep + Cook Time: 3 hours

Crust Type: Light

Program: French

Ingredients:

- 4 cups (520 g) all-cause flour

- ½ cup (100 and twenty ml) water

- ½ cup (120 ml) milk

- 2 entire eggs, overwhelmed

- ½ cup walnut (after the beep)
- 1 Tbsp. Vegetable oil
- 1 Tbsp. Sugar
- 1 tsp. Sea salt
- 1 tsp. Bread tool yeast

Nutritional Contents (constant with serving):

Total Carbs: 40g, Fiber: 1g, Protein: 9g, Fat: 7g, Calories: 257

☐Milk Wheat Bread

Prep + Cook Time: 3½ hours

Program: Basic

Crust: Medium

Yields: 2 pounds/16 slices

Ingredients

- 5¼ cups (700 g) all-reason flour
- 1¼ cups (3 hundred ml, 9½ ounces..) milk
- 2 Tbsp. Butter, softened
- 1 Tbsp. Sugar

- 2 tsp. Sea salt

- 2 tsp. Energetic dry yeast

Nutrition statistics (constant with serving)

Calories 352; Total Fat 4.5g; Saturated Fat 2.4g; Cholesterol 11g; Sodium 622mg; Total Carbohydrate sixty six.4g; Dietary Fiber 2.4g; Total Sugars 3.4g; Protein 10.1g

☐Bran Bread

Prep + Cook Time: 3 hours

Program: Basic/White Bread/French Bread

Crust: Medium

Yields: 1½ kilos/12 slices

Ingredients

- 2½ cups (340 g) all-purpose flour

- 1 complete egg, slightly overwhelmed

- ¾ cup (40 g) bran

- 1 cup (240 ml) water

- 1 Tbsp. Olive oil

- 2 tsp. Brown sugar

- 1 tsp. Sea salt

- 1 tsp. Energetic dry yeast

Nutrition information (everyday with serving)

Calories 307; Total Fat 5.1g; Saturated Fat zero.9g; Cholesterol 33g; Sodium 480mg; Total Carbohydrate 54g; Dietary Fiber 7.9g; Total Sugars 1.8g; Protein 10.2g

☐Wheat Bread with Delicate Crust

Prep + Cook Time: 3½ hours

Program: Basic

Crust: Medium

Yields: 2 pounds/16 slices

Ingredients

- 5¼ cups (seven hundred g) all-purpose flour

- 1¼ cups (three hundred ml, 9½ oz.) milk

- 2 Tbsp. Olive oil

- 2 Tbsp. Bitter cream

- 1 Tbsp. Sugar

- 2 tsp. Sea salt

- 2 tsp. Active dry yeast

Nutrition records (consistent with serving)

Calories 344; Total Fat four.9g; Saturated Fat 1.2g; Cholesterol 1g; Sodium 585mg; Total Carbohydrate sixty 4.6g; Dietary Fiber 2.4g; Total Sugars 1.7g; Protein 8.9g

☐ Honey Wheat Bread

Yield: 1½ kilos / 12 slices

Prep + Cook Time: 3 hours

Crust Type: Medium

Program: Basic/White Bread

Ingredients:

- ½ cup (100 twenty ml) water at eighty°F (27°C)

- ¼ cup (60 ml) milk at 80°F (27°C)

129

- 2 tsp. Melted butter, cooled
- 2 Tbsp. Honey
- 1 Tbsp. Molasses
- 1 tsp. Sugar
- 1 Tbsp. Skim milk powder
- ½ tsp. Salt
- 1 tsp. Unsweetened cocoa powder
- 1¼ cups (one hundred seventy g) complete-wheat flour
- 1 cup (a hundred thirty g) white bread flour
- 1 tsp. Instant yeast

Nutritional Contents (regular with serving):

Total Carbs: 34g, Fiber: 2g, Protein: 4, Fat: 2g, Calories: 164

☐ Sweet Sour Maple Bread

Yield: 1 pound / eight slices

Prep + Cook Time: three hours

Crust Type: Medium

Program: Basic/White Bread

Ingredients:

- 6 Tbsp. Water at eighty°F (27°C)

- 6 Tbsp. Bitter cream

- 1½ Tbsp. Butter, at room temperature

- ¾ Tbsp. Maple syrup

- ½ tsp. Sea salt

- 1¾ cups (230 g) all-reason flour

- 1 tsp. Bread device yeast

Nutritional Contents (consistent with serving):

Total Carbs: 31g, Fiber: 3g, Protein: 4g, Fat: 11g, Calories: 231

☐ Bran Packed Healthy Bread

Yield: 1 pound / 8 slices

Prep + Cook Time: three hours

Crust Type: Light

Program: Basic/White Bread

Ingredients:

- ¾ cup (one hundred eighty ml) milk at 80°F (27°C)
- 1½ Tbsp. Melted butter, cooled
- 2 Tbsp. Sugar
- 1 tsp. Sea salt
- ¼ cup wheat bran
- 1¾ cups (230 g) white bread flour
- 1 tsp. Immediate yeast

Nutritional Contents (consistent with serving):

Total Carbs: 26g, Fiber: 1g, Protein: 4g, Fat: 4g, Calories: 149

▯▯▯▯▯▯▯   -Honeyed

Yield: 1½ pounds / 12 slices

Prep + Cook Time: 3½ hours

Crust Type: Medium

Program: Basic/White Bread

Ingredients:

- 2¼ cups (300 g) all-purpose flour
- ¼ cup (35 g) rye flour
- 1 cup (240 ml) water
- 1 entire egg, overwhelmed
- 1 Tbsp. Vegetable oil
- 1 tsp. Sea salt
- 1½ Tbsp. Liquid honey
- 1 tsp. Lively dry yeast

Nutritional Contents (in step with serving):

Total Carbs: 33g, Fiber: 1g, Protein: 6g, Fat: 3g, Calories: 177

Spice & ☐ Herb Bread

Awesome Rosemary

Prep + Cook Time: 3½ hours

Crust Type: Medium

Program: Basic/White Bread

Ingredients:

For 1 pound / eight slices

- ¾ cup + 1 Tbsp. (two hundred ml) water at eighty°F (27°C)
- 1⅔ Tbsp. Melted butter, cooled
- 2 tsp. Sugar
- 1 tsp. Salt
- 1 Tbsp. Sparkling rosemary, chopped
- 2 cups (270 g) white bread flour
- 1⅓ tsp. On the spot yeast

For 1½ kilos / 12 slices

- 1¼ cup (300 ml) water at eighty°F (27°C)
- 2½ Tbsp. Melted butter, cooled
- 1 Tbsp. Sugar
- 1½ tsp. Salt
- 1½ Tbsp. Fresh rosemary, chopped
- 3 cups (4 hundred g) white bread flour
- 2 tsp. Instantaneous yeast

Nutritional Contents (consistent with serving):

Total Carbs: 25g, Fiber: 1g, Protein: 4g, Fat: 3g, Calories: 142

Lovely Aromatic

Prep + Cook Time: three hours

Crust Type: Medium

Program: Basic/White Bread

Ingredients:

For 1 pound / eight slices

• ¾ cup (one hundred eighty ml) milk at 80°F (27°C)

• 1 Tbsp. Melted butter, cooled

• 1 Tbsp. Sugar

• ¾ tsp. Sea salt

• 1 tsp. Clean lavender flora, chopped (after the beep)

• ¼ tsp. Lemon zest (after the beep)

• ¼ tsp. Sparkling thyme, chopped (after the beep)

• 2 cups (270 g) white bread flour

• ¾ tsp. Immediately yeast

For 1½ kilos / 12 slices

• 1 cup + 1 Tbsp. (270 ml) milk at eighty°F (27°C)

• 1½ Tbsp. Melted butter, cooled

• 1½ Tbsp. Sugar

• 1 tsp. Sea salt

• 2 tsp. Clean lavender flora, chopped (after the beep)

• ½ tsp. Lemon zest (after the beep)

• ½ tsp. Fresh thyme, chopped (after the beep)

• 3 cups (four hundred g) white bread flour

• 1 tsp. Instantaneous yeast

Nutritional Contents (consistent with serving):

Total Carbs: 27g, Fiber: 1g, Protein: 4g, Fat: 2g, Calories: one hundred forty four

☐ Mustard Beer Bread

Prep + Cook Time: 3½ hours

Program: Basic

Crust: Medium

Yields: 2 pounds/16 slices

Ingredients

- four cups (550 g) all-motive flour
- 1¼ cup (10 oz.., 3 hundred ml) dark beer
- 3 Tbsp. Granular mustard
- 1 tsp. Dijon mustard
- 1 Tbsp. Butter, softened
- 1 Tbsp. Black molasses
- 1 tsp. Sea salt
- 1 tsp. Active dry yeast

Nutrition information (in keeping with serving)

Calories 284; Total Fat three.3g; Saturated Fat 1.1g; Cholesterol 4g; Sodium 305mg; Total Carbohydrate fifty two.5g; Dietary Fiber 2.4g; Total Sugars 1.9g; Protein 7.9g

Crunchy Wheat

Yield: 1½ kilos / 12 slices

Prep + Cook Time: three hours

Crust Type: Medium

Program: Basic/White Bread

Ingredients:

- 1¼ cups (three hundred ml) water
- 1½ cups (two hundred g) bread flour
- 1½ cups (two hundred g) whole wheat flour
- 2 Tbsp. Sugar
- 2 Tbsp. Dry milk
- 2 Tbsp. Butter, softened
- 1½ tsp. Sea salt
- 1½ tsp. Dried basil leaves
- 1 tsp. Dried thyme leaves
- 2 tsp. Bread device yeast
- ½ cup dry roasted sunflower seeds (after the beep)

Nutritional Contents (regular with serving):

Total Carbs: 28g, Fiber: 1g, Protein: 6g, Fat: 5g, Calories: one hundred seventy

Bread Spicy Hot Red

Yield: 1 pound / 8 slices

Prep + Cook Time: 3 hours

Crust Type: Medium

Program: Basic/White Bread

Ingredients:

• ¾ cup + 1 Tbsp. Milk at room temperature

• 3 Tbsp. Red pepper experience (after the beep)

• 4 tsp. Chopped roasted purple pepper (after the beep)

• 2 Tbsp. Melted butter, cooled

• 2 Tbsp. Light brown sugar

• 2/3 tsp. Sea salt

• 2 cups (270 g) white bread flour

• 1 tsp. Bread tool yeast

Nutritional Contents (consistent with serving):

Total Carbs: 28g, Fiber: 2g, Protein: 4g, Fat: 4g, Calories: 167

☐ Honey Lavender Bread

Yield: 2 pounds / 16 slices

Prep + Cook Time: 3½ hours

Crust Type: Medium

Program: Basic/White Bread

Ingredients:

- 1½ cups (200 g) wheat flour
- 2⅓ cups (3 hundred g) wholemeal flour
- 1 tsp. Clean yeast
- 1½ (360 ml) cups water
- 1 tsp. Dried lavender (after the beep)
- ½ cup walnuts, chopped (after the beep)
- 1½ Tbsp. Honey
- 1 tsp. Sea salt

Nutritional Contents (steady with serving):

Total Carbs: 46g, Fiber: 1g, Protein: 7.5g, Fat: 1.5g, Calories: 226

Mustard Beer Bread

Prep + Cook Time: 3 hours

Program: Basic

Crust: Dark

Yields: 1½ pounds/12 slices

Ingredients

• 2 1/three cups (three hundred g) all-motive flour

• ¾ cup (a hundred g) complete meal flour

• 1¼ cups (3 hundred ml) dark beer, gasoline released

• 1 Tbsp. Olive oil

• three tsp. Mustard seeds

• 2 tsp. Brown sugar

• 1 tsp. Sea salt

• 1½ tsp. Energetic dry yeast

Nutrition information (in step with serving)

Calories 118; Total Fat 1g; Saturated Fat zero.4g; Cholesterol 2g; Sodium 304mg; Total Carbohydrate 23.6g; Dietary Fiber 2.3g; Total Sugars 1.6g; Protein 4.1g

Sunflower Seed &

Yield: 1½ pounds / 12 slices

Prep + Cook Time: three hours

Crust Type: Light

Program: Basic/White Bread

Ingredients:

- 1 cup (240 ml) water
- ¼ cup honey
- 2 Tbsp. Butter, softened
- 3 cups (four hundred g) bread flour
- ½ cup brief-cooking oats
- 2 Tbsp. Dry milk

- 1¼ tsp. Sea salt
- 2¼ tsp. Bread device yeast
- ½ cup sunflower seeds (after the beep)

Nutritional Contents (steady with serving):

Total Carbs: 36g, Fiber: 1g, Protein: 6g, Fat: 5g, Calories: 2 hundred

Fragrant Cardamom

Yield: 1 pound / 8 slices

Prep + Cook Time: 3 hours

Crust Type: Medium

Program: Basic/White Bread

Ingredients:

- ½ cup (100 twenty ml) milk at eighty°F (27°C)
- 1 egg, at room temperature
- 1 tsp. Melted butter, cooled
- 4 tsp. Liquid honey
- ⅔ tsp. Sea salt

- ⅔ tsp. Floor cardamom

- 2 cups (260 g) white bread flour

- ¾ tsp. Immediately yeast

Nutritional Contents (constant with serving):

Total Carbs: 29g, Fiber: 2g, Protein: 5g, Fat: 2g, Calories: 149

Cumin Tossed

Prep + Cook Time: 3½ hours

Crust Type: Medium

Program: French Bread

Ingredients:

For 1½ pounds / 12 slices

- 3¼ cups (440 g) all-reason flour

- 1 tsp. Sea salt

- 1 Tbsp. Sugar

- 2 tsp. Active dry yeast

- 1 cup (240 ml) water

- 1½ Tbsp. Cumin

- 2 Tbsp. Sunflower oil

For 2½ pounds / 20 slices

- 5⅓ cups (730 g) all-motive flour
- 1½ tsp. Sea salt
- 1½ Tbsp. Sugar
- 1 Tbsp. Lively dry yeast
- 1¾ cups (420 ml) water
- 2 Tbsp. Cumin
- 3 Tbsp. Sunflower oil

Nutritional Contents (regular with serving):

Total Carbs: 67g, Fiber: 2g, Protein: nine.5g, Fat: 7g, Calories: 368

Homemade Omega-3 Bread

Prep + Cook Time: 3½ hours

Program: Basic

Crust: Medium

Yields: 2½ pounds/20 slices

Ingredients

- 3 cups (400 g) all-motive flour

- 1 cup (100 fifty g) flaxseed meal, soak in cool water for 1/2-hour

- three/5 cup (one hundred forty ml) milk

- ½ cup (one hundred twenty ml) lukewarm water (one hundred fifteen°F/46°C)

- 2 whole eggs, barely beaten

- 2 Tbsp. Canola oil

- three Tbsp. Flax seeds

- 1 Tbsp. Sesame seeds/sunflower seeds/poppy seeds (after the beep)

- 2 Tbsp. Sugarcane

- 2 tsp. Sea salt

- 2 tsp. Lively dry yeast

Nutrition information (according to serving)

Calories 289; Total Fat 9g; Saturated Fat 1.3g; Cholesterol 42g; Sodium 608mg; Total Carbohydrate 38.8g; Dietary Fiber 7.1g; Total Sugars 1.9g; Protein 11.1g

☐ Green Onion Bread

Yield: 1½ pounds / 12 slices

Prep + Cook Time: 3 hours

Crust Type: Medium

Program: Basic/White Bread

Ingredients:

• ½ cup inexperienced onion, sliced (after the beep)

• ½ tsp. Dried basil (after the beep)

• ½ tsp. Dried thyme (after the beep)

• ¼ tsp. Dried rosemary (after the beep)

• 2 Tbsp. Butter, melted

• 1 cup (240 ml) milk

• 1 entire egg, barely beaten

• 2 Tbsp. Sugar

• ¾ tsp. Sea salt

• three cups (four hundred g) bread flour

• 2 tsp. Lively dry yeast

147

Nutrition information (consistent with serving)

Total Carbs: 27g, Fiber: 2g, Protein: 3g, Fat: 4g, Calories: 161

Anise Lemon Bread

Yield: 1 pound / eight slices

Prep + Cook Time: three hours

Crust Type: Medium

Program: Basic/White Bread

Ingredients:

- ⅔ cup (160 ml) water at 80°F (27°C)
- 1 complete egg, at room temperature
- 2⅔ Tbsp. Butter, melted and cooled
- 2⅔ Tbsp. Liquid honey
- ⅓ tsp. Sea salt
- ⅔ tsp. Anise seed (after the beep)
- ⅔ tsp. Lemon zest (after the beep)

- 2 cups (260 g) white bread flour
- 1⅓ tsp. Immediately yeast

Nutritional Contents (regular with serving):

Total Carbs: 34g, Fiber: 1g, Protein: 5g, Fat: 5g, Calories: 198

Hot Paprika

Yield: 1 pound / 8 slices

Prep + Cook Time: three hours

Crust Type: Light

Program: Basic/White Bread

Ingredients:

- 1 cup (240 ml) water at room temperature
- 2 Tbsp. Butter, easy
- 1/three cup onion, finely chopped (after the beep)
- 1½ tsp. Sea salt
- 1 tsp. Sugar

- 1 tsp. Paprika

- three cups (4 hundred g) bread flour

- 1 % active dry yeast

Nutritional Contents (regular with serving):

Total Carbs: 17g, Fiber: 1g, Protein: 3g, Fat: 1g, Calories: ninety two

Cinnamon-Flavored

Yield: 1 pound / 8 slices

Prep + Cook Time: three hours

Crust Type: Medium

Program: Sweet Bread

Ingredients:

- ¾ cup (one hundred and 80 ml) milk at 80°F (27°C)

- 1 Tbsp. Melted butter, cooled

- 1 Tbsp. Sugar

- ¾ tsp. Sea salt

- ½ tsp. Ground cinnamon (after the beep)

- 2 cups (260 g) white bread flour

- 1 tsp. Immediately yeast

- ½ cup golden raisins (after the beep)

Nutritional Contents (in step with serving):

Total Carbs: 34g, Fiber: 2g, Protein: 4g, Fat: 3g, Calories: 173

☐Mustard Bread

Prep + Cook Time: three hours

Crust Type: Medium

Program: Basic/White Bread

Ingredients:

For 2½ kilos / 20 slices

- 1¼ cups (300 ml) milk

- 3 Tbsp. Sunflower oil

- 3 Tbsp. Bitter cream

- 2 Tbsp. Dry mustard

- 1 entire egg, beaten
- ½ sachet sugar vanilla
- four cups (550 g) all-cause flour
- 1 tsp. Dry yeast
- 2 Tbsp. Sugar
- 2 tsp. Sea salt

For 1½ pounds / 12 slices
- ¾ cups (100 80 ml) milk
- 2 Tbsp. Sunflower oil
- 2 Tbsp. Bitter cream
- 1 Tbsp. Dry mustard
- 1 complete egg, crushed
- ¼ sachet sugar vanilla
- 2½ cups (330 g) all-purpose flour
- 1 tsp. Dry yeast
- 1 Tbsp. Sugar
- 1 tsp. Sea salt

Nutritional Contents (consistent with serving):

Total Carbs: 54g, Fiber: 1g, Protein: 10g, Fat: 10g, Calories: 340

Cinnamon

Yield: 1 pound / 8 slices

Prep + Cook Time: 3 hours

Crust Type: Medium

Program: Basic/White Bread

Ingredients:

- ⅔ cup (a hundred and sixty ml) milk at eighty°F (27°C)

- 1 whole egg, overwhelmed

- three Tbsp. Melted butter, cooled

- ⅓ cup (eighty g) sugar

- ⅓ tsp. Sea salt

- 1 tsp. Ground cinnamon

- 2 cups (260 g) white bread flour

- 1⅓ tsp. Energetic dry yeast

Nutritional Contents (in keeping with serving):

Total Carbs: 34g, Fiber: 1g, Protein: 5g, Fat: 5g, Calories: 198

☐ Mediterranean Bread

☐

☐ Italian Semolina Bread

Prep + Cook Time: 3½ hours

Crust Type: Medium

Program: Sandwich Bread/Italian Bread

Ingredients:

For 1½ pounds / 12 slices

- 1 cup (240 ml) water

- 1 tsp. Sea salt

- 2½ Tbsp. Butter

- 2½ tsp. Sugar

- 2¼ cups (three hundred g) all-motive flour

- ⅓ cups (60 g) semolina

- 1½ tsp. Energetic dry yeast

For 2½ pounds / 20 slices

- 2 cups (480 ml) water
- 2 tsp. Sea salt
- 5 Tbsp. Butter, softened
- five tsp. Sugar
- 4½ cups (600 g) all-cause flour
- 2/three cups (100 twenty g) semolina
- three tsp. Active dry yeast

Nutritional Contents (in line with serving):

Total Carbs: 45g, Fiber: 1g, Protein: 7g, Fat: 10g, Calories: 302

Brioche

Prep + Cook Time: 3½ hours

Program: Basic

Crust: Dark

Yields: 1½ pounds/12 slices

Ingredients

- 2½ cups (350 g) bread flour

- 1/3 cup (eighty ml) lukewarm milk (one hundred fifteen°F/forty six°C)

- 2 large eggs, overwhelmed

- ½ cup (a hundred and ten g) butter, melted

- 2 Tbsp. Sugar

- 1 tsp. Sea salt

- 1½ tsp. Active dry yeast

Nutrition facts (consistent with serving)

Calories 147; Total Fat 13g; Saturated Fat 7.8g; Cholesterol 78mg; Sodium 395mg; Total Carbohydrate five.8g; Dietary Fiber 0.2g; Total Sugars three.6g; Protein 2.6g

Italian Onion

Yield: 1 pound / eight slices

Prep + Cook Time: three - four hours

Crust Type: Light

Program: Basic/White Bread

Ingredients:

- 1 cup heat milk, at room temperature
- 1 large complete egg
- 2 Tbsp. Butter, clean
- ¼ cup dried onion, minced (after the beep)
- 1½ tsp. Sea salt
- 2 Tbsp. Dried parsley flakes (after the beep)
- 1 tsp. Dried oregano (after the beep)
- 3½ cups (460 g) bread flour
- 2 tsp. Active dry yeast

Nutritional Contents (in keeping with serving):

Total Carbs: 23g, Fiber: 1g, Protein: 5g, Fat: 2g, Calories: 100 twenty 5

French Cheese Onion Bread

Prep + Cook Time: 3¾ hours

Program: French Bread

Crust: Medium

Yields: 2 pounds/16 slices

Ingredients

• 3¼ cups (450 g) all-cause flour

• 4/five cup (two hundred ml) lukewarm milk (a hundred and fifteen°F/forty six°C)

• 1 Tbsp. Olive oil

• 1 Tbsp. Butter, melted

• ½ cup (forty five g) Parmesan cheese, grated (after the beep)

• 1 onion (a hundred and ten g), chopped and fried (after the beep)

• 1¼ tsp. Sea salt

• 1 tsp. Energetic dry yeast

Nutrition records (in keeping with serving)

Calories 260; Total Fat 6.5g; Saturated Fat 3g; Cholesterol 13g; Sodium 432mg; Total Carbohydrate forty one.5g; Dietary Fiber 1.8g; Total Sugars 1.9g; Protein eight.2g

Exuberant Egg

Prep + Cook Time: 3½ hours

Crust Type: Light

Program: French Bread

Ingredients:

For 1 pound / 8 slices

- ½ cup + 2 Tbsp. (a hundred and forty ml) milk at 80°F (27°C)

- 2⅔ Tbsp. Melted butter, cooled

- 1 whole egg, overwhelmed

- 2⅔ Tbsp. Sugar

- 1 tsp. Sea salt

- 2 cups (270 g) all-cause flour

- ¾ tsp. On the spot yeast

For 2 pounds / 16 slices

- 1 1/6 cup (280 ml) milk at 80°F (27°C)

- 5 1/3 Tbsp. Melted butter, cooled

- 2 complete eggs, beaten

- five 1/three Tbsp. Sugar

- 2 tsp. Sea salt

- 4 cups (540 g) all-cause flour

- 1½ tsp. Immediate yeast

Nutritional Contents (consistent with serving):

Total Carbs: 29g, Fiber: 1g, Protein: 5g, Fat: 5g, Calories: 184

☐ Italian Onion Bread

Prep + Cook Time: 3½ hours

Program: Basic

Crust: Medium

Yields: 1½ pounds/12 slices

Ingredients

- 2½ cups (350 g) all-purpose flour

- 1 cup (240 ml) lukewarm water (115°F/forty six°C)

- three Tbsp. Olive oil

- 2 big onions (three hundred g), chopped and fried (after beeping)

- 1 Tbsp. Sugar

- 1½ tsp. Sea salt
- 1 tsp. Bread gadget yeast

Nutrition facts (consistent with serving)

Calories 209; Total Fat 5.7g; Saturated Fat 0.8g; Cholesterol 0g; Sodium 441mg; Total Carbohydrate 35g; Dietary Fiber 2g; Total Sugars three.2g; Protein four.6g

Delicious Italian

Prep + Cook Time: 3 hours

Crust Type: Medium

Program: Basic/White Bread

Ingredients:

For 1 pound / 8 slices

- ⅔ cup (160 ml) water at eighty°F (27°C)
- 1 Tbsp. Olive oil
- 1 Tbsp. Sugar
- ¾ tsp. Sea salt

- 2 cups (270 g) all-purpose flour
- 1 tsp. Immediate yeast

For 2 kilos / 16 slices

- 1 1/3 cup (320 ml) water at 80°F (27°C)
- 2 Tbsp. Olive oil
- 2 Tbsp. Sugar
- 1½ tsp. Sea salt
- 4 cups (540 g) all-purpose flour
- 2 tsp. On the spot yeast

Nutritional Contents (steady with serving):

Total Carbs: 26g, Fiber: 1g, Protein: 3g, Fat: 2g, Calories: 136

Original Italian

Prep + Cook Time: 3½ hours

Crust Type: Medium

Program: French Bread

Ingredients:

For 1½ pounds / 12 slices

- ½ cup (110 ml) water at 80°F (27°C)
- ½ cup (110 ml) olive brine
- 1 Tbsp. Butter, softened
- 2 Tbsp. Sugar
- 1 tsp. Sea salt
- three cups (430 g) all-cause flour
- 1½ tsp. Bread device yeast
- 12 olives, black/inexperienced, sliced (after the beep)
- 1 tsp. Italian herbs (after the beep)

For 2½ pounds / 20 slices

- 1 cup (240 ml) water at eighty°F (27°C)
- ½ cup (a hundred twenty ml) olive brine
- 1½ Tbsp. Butter, softened
- three Tbsp. Sugar
- 2 tsp. Sea salt
- 5⅓ cups (760 g) all-reason flour
- 2 tsp. Bread tool yeast

• 20 olives, black/green, sliced (after the beep)

• 1½ tsp. Italian herbs (after the beep)

Nutritional Contents (in keeping with serving):

Total Carbs: 71g, Fiber: 1g, Protein: 10g, Fat: 7g, Calories: 386

□Italian Tomato Cheese Bread

Prep + Cook Time: 3½ hours

Program: Basic/Italian Bread

Crust: Medium

Yields: 1½ kilos.12 slices

Ingredients

• 2½ cups (350 g) all-reason flour

• 1 cup (240 ml) lukewarm milk (a hundred and fifteen°F/46°C)

• 1 Tbsp. Olive oil

• five Tbsp. Sun-dried tomatoes (20 g), chopped (after the beep)

- ½ cup (50 g) difficult cheese, grated (after the beep)

- 1 Tbsp. Sugar

- 1½ tsp. Sea salt

- 1 tsp. Lively dry yeast

Nutrition facts (in line with serving)

Calories 209; Total Fat 5.1g; Saturated Fat 2.2g; Cholesterol 10g; Sodium 498mg; Total Carbohydrate 33.4g; Dietary Fiber 1.2g; Total Sugars three.2g; Protein 7g

Olive Bread with Italian Herbs

Prep + Cook Time: 3½ hours

Program: Basic/ Italian Bread

Crust: Medium

Yields: 2 pounds/16 slices

Ingredients

- 4 cups (550 g) all-motive flour

- 1 cup (240 ml) lukewarm water (one hundred fifteen°F/46°C)

- ½ cup (100 twenty ml) brine from olives

- four Tbsp. Softened butter

- ½ cup olives (60 g), chopped (after beeping)

- 1 tsp. Italian herbs

- 3 Tbsp. Sugar

- 2 tsp. Sea salt

- 2 tsp. Energetic dry yeast

Nutrition information (steady with serving)

Calories 332; Total Fat 7.5g; Saturated Fat 3.9g; Cholesterol 15g; Sodium 749mg; Total Carbohydrate fifty 5.5g; Dietary Fiber 3g; Total Sugars 4.8g; Protein 7.9g

Crispy French

Prep + Cook Time: 3½ hours

Crust Type: Light

Program: French Bread

Ingredients:

For 1 pound / 8 slices

• ⅔ cup (a hundred and sixty ml) water at eighty°F (27°C)

• 2 tsp. Olive oil

• 1 Tbsp. Sugar

• ⅔ tsp. Sea salt

• 2 cups (270 g) all-cause flour

• 1 tsp. Instantaneous yeast

For 2 pounds / sixteen slices

• 1 1/three cup (320 ml) water at eighty°F (27°C)

• four tsp. Olive oil

• 2 Tbsp. Sugar

• 1 tsp. Sea salt

• four cups (550 g) all-reason flour

• 2 tsp. Instant yeast

Nutritional Contents (consistent with serving):

Total Carbs: 26g, Fiber: 1g, Protein: 3g, Fat: 2g, Calories: a hundred thirty five

☐Italian Tomato Cheese Bread with Saffron

Prep + Cook Time: 3½ hours

Program: Basic/Italian Bread

Crust: Medium

Yields: 2 pounds/sixteen slices

Ingredients

- 2½ cups (350 g) all-cause flour

- 1½ cups (360 ml) serum

- 2 Tbsp. Olive oil

- 1 Tbsp. Tomato paste

- ½ cup (50 g) hard cheese, diced (after the beep)

- ½ cup (fifty five g) feta cheese (after the beep)

- 2 Tbsp. Solar-dried tomatoes, chopped (after the beep)

- 1 Tbsp. Panifarin

- 1 pinch saffron

- 1½ Tbsp. Sugar

- 1½ tsp. Sea salt

- 1 tsp. Active dry yeast

Nutrition records (regular with serving)

Calories 260; Total Fat 9.2g; Saturated Fat 4g; Cholesterol 20g; Sodium 611mg; Total Carbohydrate 35.5g; Dietary Fiber 1.3g; Total Sugars five.2g; Protein eight.9g

French Strawberry Bread

Prep + Cook Time: 4 hours

Program: French Bread

Crust: Medium

Yields: 2½ kilos/20 slices

Ingredients

- four cups (550 g) bread machine flour

- 1¾ cups (420 ml) water

- 1 cup (a hundred fifty g) sparkling strawberries, chopped (after the beep)

- three Tbsp. Sugar

- 1 tsp. Sea salt

- 1 tsp. Bread system yeast

Nutrition facts (steady with serving)

Calories 313; Total Fat 0.9g; Saturated Fat 0.1g; Cholesterol 0mg; Sodium 973g; Total Carbohydrate sixty five.7g; Dietary Fiber 2.9g; Total Sugars 1.Four g; Protein 9g

Fruity French

Yield: 1 pound / eight slices

Prep + Cook Time: 3 hours

Crust Type: Light

Program: Basic/White Bread

Ingredients:

- ¾ cup canned pears, mashed (after the beep)

- ¼ cup (60 ml) water

- 1 Tbsp. Liquid honey

- 1 egg, barely crushed

- 3 cups (4 hundred g) bread flour

- 1/eight tsp. Pepper

- 1 tsp. Energetic dry yeast

Nutritional Contents (consistent with serving):

Total Carbs: 9g, Fiber: 2g, Protein: 5g, Fat: 9g, Calories: 158

☐ Bread from Around the World

☐

☐ British Muffin Bread

Yield: 1 pound / eight slices

Prep + Cook Time: three hours

Crust Type: Medium

Program: Basic/White Bread

Ingredients:

For 1 pound / eight slices

- ⅔ cup (160 ml) buttermilk at 80°F (27°C)

- 1 Tbsp. Melted butter, cooled

- 1 Tbsp. Sugar

- ¾ tsp. Sea salt

- ¼ tsp. Baking powder

- 1¾ cups (240 g) white bread flour

- 1⅛ tsp. Instantaneous yeast

For 2 kilos / 16 slices

- 1 1/3 cup (320 ml) buttermilk at 80°F (27°C)

- 2 Tbsp. Melted butter, cooled

- 2 Tbsp. Sugar

- 1 tsp. Sea salt

- ½ tsp. Baking powder

- 3½ cups (480 g) white bread flour

- 2 tsp. Immediate yeast

Nutritional Contents (consistent with serving):

Total Carbs: 24g, Fiber: 2g, Protein: 4g, Fat: 2g, Calories: 131

☐ Traditional Japanese White Bread

Prep + Cook Time: 3½ hours

Program: Basic/White bread

Crust: Medium

Yields: 1½ kilos/12 slices

Ingredients

• 3½ cups (450 g) all-motive flour

• ½ cup (100 twenty ml) lukewarm milk (one hundred fifteen°F/forty six°C)

• 1 cup (240 ml) lukewarm water (one hundred fifteen°F/forty six°C)

• 2 Tbsp. Sugar

• 1 Tbsp. Butter, softened

• 1 tsp. Kosher salt

• 2 Tbsp. Bread gadget yeast

Nutrition information (regular with serving)

Calories 240; Total Fat 2.4g; Saturated Fat 1.2g; Cholesterol 5g; Sodium 312mg; Total Carbohydrate 46.6g; Dietary Fiber 2.1g; Total Sugars 3.8g; Protein 7.3g

☐ Sweet Challah

Yield: 1½ kilos / 12 slices

Prep + Cook Time: 3 hours

Crust Type: Light

Program: Basic/White Bread

Ingredients:

- ¾ cup (one hundred eighty ml) milk
- 2 entire eggs, slightly beaten
- 3 Tbsp. Margarine
- three cups (four hundred g) bread flour
- ¼ cup (60 g) white sugar
- 1½ tsp. Sea salt
- 1½ tsp. Lively dry yeast

Nutritional Contents (in step with serving):

Total Carbs: 30g, Fiber: 1g, Protein: 6g, Fat: 4g, Calories: 184

☐ German Bread Linz

Prep + Cook Time: 3½ hours

Program: Basic/ Rye Bread

Crust: Medium

Yields: 2 pounds/16 slices

Ingredients

- 2¼ cups (3 hundred g) rye flour

- 2¼ cups (three hundred g) wheat flour

- 1½ cups (360 ml) water

- 2 whole eggs, slightly overwhelmed

- 2 Tbsp. Olive oil

- 2 Tbsp. Liquid honey

- 2 tsp. Sea salt

- 2 tsp. Active dry yeast

Nutrition data (in step with serving)

Calories 309; Total Fat 6g; Saturated Fat 1g; Cholesterol 41g; Sodium 600mg; Total Carbohydrate 56.4g; Dietary Fiber 9.3g; Total Sugars 4.9g; Protein 10.5g

Swiss Whole Meal Cheese Bread

Prep + Cook Time: three hours

Program: Basic

Crust: Dark

Yields: 1 pound/eight slices

Ingredients

• 1 cup (one hundred forty g) all-purpose flour

• 9/10 cup (120 g) whole-grain flour

• ¾ cup (a hundred 80 ml) lukewarm water (115°F/46°C)

• 2 Tbsp. Blue cheese (after the beep)

• 1 tsp. Paprika (after the beep)

• 1 Tbsp. Sugar

• 1 tsp. Sea salt

• 1 tsp. Bread device yeast

Nutrition facts (in keeping with serving)

Calories 118; Total Fat 1g; Saturated Fat zero.4g; Cholesterol 2g; Sodium 304mg; Total Carbohydrate 23.6g; Dietary Fiber 2.3g; Total Sugars 1.6g; Protein 4.1g

☐ Greek Olive Bread

Prep + Cook Time: 3½ hours

Program: Basic

Crust: Medium

Yields: 2½ kilos/20 slices

Ingredients

- four cups (550 g) all-motive flour

- 1½ cups (360 ml) water

- 3 Tbsp. Olive oil

- 1 cup (one hundred thirty g) olives, sliced (after the beep)

- 1 Tbsp. Sugar

- 1½ tsp. Sea salt

- 1 tsp. Active dry yeast

Nutrition facts (according to serving)

Calories 299; Total Fat 7.7g; Saturated Fat 1.1g; Cholesterol 0g; Sodium 587mg; Total Carbohydrate 50.4g; Dietary Fiber 2.3g; Total Sugars 1.7g; Protein 6.8g

☐ Traditional English Bread

Prep + Cook Time: 3½ hours

Program: Basic

Crust: Medium

Yields: 2½ kilos/20 slices

Ingredients

• 4½ cups (600 g) all-motive flour

• ½ cup (eighty g) polenta

• 2 cups (480 ml) lukewarm water (one hundred fifteen°F/forty six°C)

• five Tbsp. (ninety g) molasses

- 2 tsp. Lemon juice

- 3 Tbsp. Melted butter

- 2½ tsp. Sea salt

- 2 tsp. Active dry yeast

Nutrition statistics (regular with serving)

Calories 368; Total Fat 5.2g; Saturated Fat 2.9g; Cholesterol 11g; Sodium 767mg; Total Carbohydrate 71g; Dietary Fiber 2.4g; Total Sugars 7.3g; Protein eight.4g

Italian Bread Pan Marino

Prep + Cook Time: 3½ hours

Program: Basic

Crust: Medium

Yields: 2 pounds/sixteen slices

Ingredients

- 3½ cups (480 g) all-reason flour

- 1 cup (240 ml) lukewarm water (115°F/forty six°C)

- 2 Tbsp. Milk powder

- 2 Tbsp. Olive oil

- 2 Tbsp. Clean rosemary, chopped (after the beep)

- 1 Tbsp. Sugarcane

- 1 tsp. Sea salt

- 1 tsp. Active dry yeast

Nutrition data (consistent with serving)

Calories 246; Total Fat four.2g; Saturated Fat 0.6g; Cholesterol 0g; Sodium 248mg; Total Carbohydrate 45g; Dietary Fiber 1.9g; Total Sugars 2.7g; Protein 6.6g

Spicy Hawaiian

Prep + Cook Time: 3½ hours

Program: Basic

Yield: 2 kilos / sixteen slices

Ingredients:

- 1¼ cups (three hundred ml) milk
- 1 Tbsp. Vanilla extract
- ¼ cup (60 g) brown sugar
- 2 Tbsp. Granulated sugar
- 1¼ tsp. Sea salt
- ¼ tsp. Ground coriander (after the beep)
- 1/8 tsp. Floor cardamom (after the beep)
- 2 Tbsp. Butter, melted
- 3½ cups (480 g) bread flour
- 1 percent speedy rise yeast

Nutritional Contents (regular with serving):

Total Carbs: 7g, Fiber: 1g, Protein: 1g, Fat: 3g, Calories: fifty seven

☐ Italian Raisin Rosemary Bread

Prep + Cook Time: 3½ hours

Program: Basic

Crust: Medium

Yields: 2 pounds/16 slices

Ingredients

- 3 cups (4 hundred g) bread machine flour

- ¾ cup (a hundred 80 ml) lukewarm water (a hundred and fifteen°F/46°C)

- 2 entire eggs, slightly beaten

- 4 Tbsp. Olive oil

- 3 Tbsp. Rosemary, freshly chopped (after the beep)

- 1 cup (a hundred forty five g) raisins (after the beep)

- small sprigs of rosemary, for adornment

- 1 Tbsp. Sugar

- 1 tsp. Sea salt

- 1 tsp. Energetic dry yeast

Nutrition records (in keeping with serving)

Calories 312; Total Fat eight.8g; Saturated Fat 1.5g; Cholesterol forty one; Sodium 311mg;

Total Carbohydrate 52.7g; Dietary Fiber 2.6g; Total Sugars 12.4g; Protein 7g

☐ French Ham Bread

Prep + Cook Time: 3½ hours

Program: French Bread

Crust: Medium

Yields: 2 kilos/sixteen slices

Ingredients

- 3 1/three cups (450 g) all-purpose flour
- 1 1/three cups (320 ml) lukewarm water (one hundred fifteen°F/forty six°C)
- 1 cup (134 g) ham, chopped (after the beep)
- 2 Tbsp. Olive oil
- ½ cup (sixty 5 g) milk powder
- 1 tsp. Dried basil (after the beep)
- 1 ½ Tbsp. Sugar

- 1 tsp. Sea salt
- 1 tsp. Clean yeast

www.ingramcontent.com/pod-product-compliance
Lightning Source LLC
Chambersburg PA
CBHW071332120626
46546CB00002B/537